MESSAGES

FLOWING WITH SYNCHRONICITY

To Charlie —
a master who heals
himself and therefore
the planet.

Denny Daikeler

DENNY DAIKELER

BALBOA.
PRESS
A DIVISION OF HAY HOUSE

Cover Art: Mary Myrka
Photographer: Christopher John

Balboa Press books may be ordered through booksellers or by contacting:

Balboa Press
A Division of Hay House
1663 Liberty Drive
Bloomington, IN 47403
www.balboapress.com
1-(877) 407-4847

ISBN: 978-1-4525-4323-9 (sc)
ISBN: 978-1-4525-4325-3 (hc)
ISBN: 978-1-4525-4324-6 (e)

Library of Congress Control Number: 2011961410

The author of this book does not dispense medical advice or prescribe the use of any technique as a form of treatment for physical, emotional, or medical problems without the advice of a physician, either directly or indirectly. The intent of the author is only to offer information of a general nature to help you in your quest for emotional and spiritual well-being. In the event you use any of the information in this book for yourself, which is your constitutional right, the author and the publisher assume no responsibility for your actions.

Any people depicted in stock imagery provided by Thinkstock are models, and such images are being used for illustrative purposes only.
Certain stock imagery © Thinkstock.

Printed in the United States of America

Balboa Press rev. date: 03/28/2012

Dedicated to my soul sister
Barbara Reid
Because of our relationship around all this wonder
And because she insisted I write
these stories down!

I am so grateful!

And to my Blessed Grandchildren

Josef Jagger May
Ava Delaney Daikeler
Christian David Daikeler
Daniel David Daikeler
Damien Rishel
Alison Zywalewski
Nicolas Zywalewski

ACKNOWLEDGEMENTS

I hesitate to write this page. I fear I'll forget someone very important. Some friends that I list won't understand their existence on this page. To help them I'll say this list is to honor persons in my life who have influenced this work just by being who they are, by what they believe, how they live, risk, explore, and expand. Their way of being has helped me write these stories down, and to expand myself. There is my family, who have been willing to listen to these stories as they happened, and to love and believe in me all the same! Thank you Robin, Carl and David, Ken, Isabelle and Julie, Ray and my brother Ken. Thank you Barbara Reid for your willingness to listen. Rene Ragan for your wonderful editing, Rick Ragan, David Lello and John Sandy, Gary Culp, my dancing partner, Bill Ehrich, Melinda Bergen, Liz Theodore, Marie Woody, Neelie Theis, Carley and Hannah Theis, Linda Timpone, Fran Grabowski, Curt and Beverly Weihz, Connie and Ned Woody, Hannalore Goodwin, Bunny Dodd, Rabbi Michael Shevack, Renee Welde, Gordon and Gayle Dragt, Claire and Joe Billingham, Kate White and Brad Holbrook. Thank you my dear Jonathon and Kacey Daly, Alex and Allyson Grey, and my beloved Intenders Group.

Thank you Mary Myrka for your wonderful art for the cover.
Thank you Christopher John,
for your incredible photography of Mary's art.
And thank you Universe. You created this and the experience
has made my life expand.
I am blessed.

CONTENTS

TABLE OF EXERCISES

INTRODUCTION

When we are ready the teacher comes . . .
And then the challenge comes . . .
Will you open to the possibility?

The sun was just coming up as I was prepared to leave for Los Angeles, for two weeks of R&R! My last week had been long, and the weather in Philadelphia was cold with temperatures in the 20's. None of it was an issue now. I had my book, new digs and I was on my way.

I arrived at the airport early, with many empty seats at the gate. In no time I was on the plane with my watch set for California time. As the plane lifted into the air, my feelings soared. Within minutes our altitude leveled off and suddenly it was as if I was in a new dimension. My mind was filled with memories, familiar stories of encounters and synchronicities that had happened to me over the last fifteen or so years. I didn't fight their presence. I was amused. It was precious to remember them again. I smiled visualizing, the owl on the branch and the snake at the side of my foot...but let me catch you up.

I've been a student of Philosophy and Theology really all my life. Just like you I've sought the meaning of life, the brilliant wonderings and wanderings of great sages. I've read all the masters over and over, and even managed to be ordained as an Interfaith Minister in 2001. But simple and mystical encounters with owls and snakes and such were beginning to happen to me, and they challenged my beliefs as well as my acceptance of the written word over the personal experience. These "teachers" (yes, the owls and snakes!) showed up more frequently as I began respecting them and listening to their messages. Sometimes I felt a bit crazy with what was happening to me, and what I was thinking. Or perhaps I felt foolish? Day after day there were nudges instructing me to pay attention to and question everything. I felt very puzzled. Repetitive encounters with an owl finally convinced me that I was being encouraged to wake up! "But to what?" I thought.

I've only shared these stories with a few friends, those who would "understand," if you know what I mean. Each time I shared I got a new insight that moved me to change my beliefs, question my choices, and wonder about reality big time! I'd often thought of recording them, but I just never took the time. What I didn't know about this particular day was the universe had decided this was the time. Six hours in a plane! A Direct flight! PERFECT! I could literally hear the universe saying," She's put it off long enough!

"I want you to know that I'd held these stories very sacred for years. In fact their occurrences had changed my life. In this moment I was enchanted with beginning to write them down. For the next six hours as we flew through the beautiful blue skies going west, I began this book. The first draft of chapter one was finished when we landed in LA. I got so engrossed that I wrote for many afternoons of my vacation. I saw how to organize my stories, what to emphasize, and how to make them alive for you. It was dawn at the end of a glorious two weeks when I was preparing to leave for home that an owl began hooting off in the distance. I had never heard an owl in LA before! I put down my suitcase, closed my eyes, and gave thanks for what I knew was coming to pass. I knew I'd fulfilled a big desire by beginning, and I knew I was following my own personal Truth

These stories hold my new belief that all of our experience is our soul evolving us from darkness to Light. No person and no event are excluded. We are in a transformational process. We can keep it happening through questioning, listening, knowing and changing, and we can slow it down over lifetimes by going to sleep and not doing the work. In this life process we are tapped on the shoulder constantly. That tap is our soul attempting this evolution of ours. How much we listen and respond is up to us.

The way I now see it is this soul of ours is conspiring with our external world to try to tell us our personal Truth, or our next step. It pulls us along, and as that is happening, in step the troops, a most amazing family of guides, synchronicities, totems, and angels in all forms, just for us. Along side are our own personal feelings that are practically shouting (if we're listening!) what to do, where to go, and how to do it! It's all toward our greatest good, our own enlightenment. Our messages may not get in because of resistance, limiting beliefs, grief, anger, fear or limited thinking. If we accept that and open, we have the chance to grow. I humbly offer these tales of my waking up, as an example of your soul's guidance. I also, include exercises at the end of each chapter that may help the process of clearing away your issues. With each clearing will come an ability to hear more of your soul's precious voice.

If you have found yourself yearning for more, wanting your days to be richer, your beliefs to go deeper, then you are ready for this book. Let the stories entertain you and at the same time open your mind and help you chart your path.

Paulo Coelho writes in his book, The Valkeyries, that we, at this moment in history, must develop and learn to make our own choices, develop our own powers. We must believe that the universe doesn't end at the walls of our room. And we must accept the signs, and follow our heart and our dreams. What an amazing journey we are all on publicly and privately... TOGETHER!

CHAPTER ONE

Asking

The constant experience of the universe through numerous instances of what seems like chance, or amazing coincidence can be traced back to you, what your thoughts have been. It all will finally bring about a feeling of wonder, certainty, gratitude, and finally joy!

My first beautiful story is the story of a Great Horned Owl. I'd often heard owls hooting in the woods surrounding the house. in the woods surrounding my home. Their piercing sound would sometimes wake me up from a sound sleep in the middle of the night, or sometimes in the early morning. Often I'd hear their hoot at the end of a day just after the trees had made long shadows across my yard. Whenever there were owls hooting, it caught my attention.

I really yearned to see these owls. Their songs seemed so haunting to me, and I loved when one owl's hoot would be answered by another. I knew they must be speaking to each other. Whether I heard one or two, I'd listen carefully to try to decide the place where I'd find them. Then I'd race to every window hoping the owl or owls would be there. Over and over again I'd make this wild dash. It was like a ritual. I'd hear the signal, listen, guess and then run for the successful sighting sure that they'd leave before I'd get there. Over and over again I would find the tree branches bare, no owlish form appearing singing its reverie. But yes, I could still hear their song.

This quest went on for so long and was sometimes frustrating and sometimes humorous. My efforts didn't payoff.

Through all of this I felt some form of the Divine. There seemed to be some message lurking in the shadows for me, and I wanted to know what the message was. I felt such a desire to SEE THIS CREATURE. Hearing it was just not enough. And I really wanted to believe that I could make this happen.

Finally one morning at dawn, I again heard "this rooster" call from the limb on some tree, at some side of the house. This time I did not spring out of my bed to frantically search every window to catch its presence. Instead I simply ASKED. I sat up in bed and asked to see the owl. "I want to see the owl," I said. "I want to see the owl!"

In that moment I must admit there truly came to me a knowing that sooner or later the owl would present itself to me. I might again franticly pursue the silhouette through the branches, but I was in a new place with this game. There was a new "knowing" that putting out my desire and then trusting was a huge step forward, one that could unlock this mystery forever.

I don't know how long it took for the owl to come to me. I did not journal and date my request. But one morning before the sun was up, as I was beginning to start my day, I heard a great deal of noise outside. I ignored it at first for I was busy and distracted. The clamor persisted growing louder and more piercing all the time. Suddenly I stopped and just opened to it. "What's going on?" I thought. "That is such a racket! Some very agitated crows must be robbing a nest of its eggs."

And then all of the sudden I knew I was being called! I knew the owl was there. I raced to the window with great excitement and confidence. And there it was high up on a branch in a tree nearby. It was huge!

It was a magnificent Great Horned Owl sitting very still and profound, looking right down at me. I tell you my world stopped. Moments seemed to stretch and grow as if they were hours as I communed with this beloved bird. My head felt like it was spinning. My eyes were struggling as if they were cameras trying to record everything, every detail. The two of us were transfixed¼ and then we were complete. Slowly, carefully, deliberately it opened its wings to the widest expanse I could have imagined and lifted itself away to the sky.

Well, the moment ended, and I knew it was a birth for me, and a communion of the highest sort. I had discovered new possibilities. My hidden belief in limitation was both revealed and banished, the one that says that only we humans can relate to each other or hear each other, that owls and other birds are just beautiful beings with wings and songs that decorate our world, reproduce, and hold in balance the food chain. Owls were teaching me.

They were like gifts, possible companions, messengers, God filled entities. Somehow out in space or no space, this creature had heard me, and it had come to me in response to my request.

My new approach to receiving what I wanted was now quite different, more like a command, or clear intention. It really felt like a dance. Its first step began the moment I stopped searching for the owls. I see my intention to wait. I asked for what I wanted. It held a feeling of patience and confidence (and even contentment!) that accompanied the asking. I didn't know what was going to happen or how it was going to happen. My yearning was also important. My hope for some connection with this other world. I wanted to believe in that connection and my power to make it happen. Maybe it wasn't even another world. But that's how it seemed to me.

An Appendix to serve you

Sometimes we just want to read some stories and relax. Sometimes we really want to dig in and make the reading a project, a journey that helps us with new thinking, new information, and new ways of being. If your goal is travelling your own spiritual path as you read MESSAGES, then I will share with you some of the tools I used to steady myself and maneuver about. As I began my journey, I knew I was being faced with my own limitations. Finding the next place to step or what to do was a challenge. A spiritual practice became my intention, and the appendix at the end of the book describes the tools I used. You may want to explore the **APPENDIX** material now so you are aware of some tools that can assist you. (It's also a fun read)

CHAPTER TWO

Listening And Knowing

Let none of the work you do on yourself
Be because of your desire for praise,
or money, or awards.
Let it come from your deepest desire
For life to be juicy, profound
And filled with Truth, your Truth!

So owls began drawing me into what seemed like another world, and into new possibilities of communicating with that world and its' creatures (at least those that had wings.) I was becoming aware that they could be my teachers. It was eerie how I sensed that they knew my comings and goings, my life with my own species, and my need to grow

Can you imagine it? I'd walk out of my door, and I could feel them aware that I was there. I'd think about something and feel they're awareness present. But I'm way ahead of my story again.

Just so you know, I was becoming very watchful and grateful of whatever was unfolding.

Shortly after that first story I had another encounter with the owl. It was a sunny morning, quite balmy with more foliage on the trees and bushes. The bare branches were gone, so I'll guess it was about a month later.

I had been enjoying the owls' hooting, but I rarely dashed for a sighting and instead was taking in the owl's presence with a feeling of trust. I considered their hoot as a soft call of love. It would make me smile or remind me of their presence nearby, or something I needed to be doing. On this particular morning I decided to meditate on the deck off my bedroom. It was about 9 AM.

Settling in I got very comfortable on my soft blanket and cushion. The air was nice. I began to listen to my breath. Suddenly my eyes popped open. I was facing east and in my line of sight was a strip of wild raspberry bushes already beginning to show signs of budding. Without any indication I KNEW as well as I know my name, that there was an owl in the bushes. Do owls hang in bushes? I didn't know. But I knew without a doubt that an owl was there. There was no rustling, no hoot, no indication. But I had this uncanny knowing that the owl was there, an owl in the brush, and it wanted me to know it was there without hearing or seeing. I can tell you that my knowing was only through a sense of its presence. It made me laugh. I was going to owl school! They now were teaching me how to "feel" knowing with deep confidence.

Well, first came knowing and then came seeing. The owl emerged with great energy; its' huge wings flapping. It flew straight toward me at a steady pace. I was taken aback by its directness and still felt what I might call communion rather than fear. And again the earth was standing still. It did not hesitate nor swerve in its mission. It passed right by my shoulder only inches away. I could feel the whisper of air from it's wings. Oh my!

I remained still but trembling a bit. It really was sweet I tell you and so exciting. I felt so many feelings of wonder, awe, joy, harmony. Whew! I loved it. The animal kingdom that I'd always adored seemed personally in relationship with me.

I remained still and awed in that spot for a long time. The adventure kept repeating itself over and over in my mind. Nothing had ever flown toward me that deliberately before. Oh, maybe a fly or a bee, but nothing large, like an owl! It did not need to repeat its passage. My imagination was doing that. I recreated the scene over and over for hours and days on end. My heart would beat in concert with the memory. I became preoccupied with what it was about and remembering what it had felt like, or even just that it had happened. My life was filled up with it . . . filled, filled, filled.

I got the message. I knew that my work now was to practice knowing, to become aware through my intuition of what I could not see. I'd try to intuit bad traffic while driving, or who was calling on the phone before I'd answer. It didn't always work, but I still knew that was my assignment. Along with that I was struggling with this new reality that was pushing at my "old ways of being." I was relating with another kingdom! Could I accept this with my linear mind that had always trusted things lining up with logic and reason? How was I to become grounded in this new reality? I shivered often when I'd think about it. What was happening? But then I'd grin for I definitely began to sense the power and even fun of all of this in my life.

Would I have ever signed up for this course? I don't think I would have even understood what it was about. But I was taking it none-the-less, and my curious mind was keeping it happening. I was becoming sensitized, waiting, waiting for the next thing. I began to know I could call the owl to my yard by thinking the words. As I had more encounters with the owls I began to hear messages as if these beings were speaking to me. Communication was often in direct relationship to my life and what was going on in it.

Then came a time when two or three owls began appearing together. They would position themselves at the end of a corridor formed by trees directly beyond my bedroom window, always on the same branches. They would line up in a very majestic formation.

One time I was about to go on vacation. It was a favorite trip that happened every year with my family. We'd go to Canada and stay in a cabin on a lake. The evening of my departure all three owls showed up. They stayed on the branches for a long time as I sat on my bed in front of the window. Their message was "Travel well! Enjoy it all. Be free in your life. You are safe!" Did I hear their voices. No. I just knew what they were saying.

It seemed as though they stayed until they were sure I'd gotten their message. Then off they flew one by one. It gave me such an affectionate feeling in my heart. I felt a warm feeling of love and an amazing message of caring. I knew I would enjoy my precious family in this time away, but the truth was that my family was growing, and it now consisted of beautiful, feathery friends. What a blessing to my life. I was beginning to see how unlimited we all are most of the time, and we don't know it. Also, I could see how my life was opening up because of a momentary, spontaneous decision to ask for what I wanted.

Everything seemed to come from the simplicity of that moment. My question, my asking to see the owl was such a turnstile. It was a journey that expanded me into an awareness of an unlimited universe. I was getting closer to understanding, and I knew it. I was pregnant with desire, and vowed to keep asking. But I will tell you that there came moments when it was hardly a conscious choice. The universe knew that I wanted more and just kept bringing it on.

Exercise
Going to a Museum

This exercise is to help you develop your knowing. It is a fabulous exercise! Please do it! Do it more than once! Do it often.

Go to a museum, any museum. Go alone, or with someone else, but walk the many halls and exhibits taking in the art, alone. Or, just don't talk to your companion. Observe and feel the art with curiosity and appreciation. Stay very open.

Begin to notice the art that seems to resonate for you, the pieces that hold you, speak to you, or that you feel connected to, that really grabs you. In other words work more at appreciating what you enjoy rather than attempting to learn about the artist or the art. When you feel saturated, go back to the ones that have remained prominent in your experience, deciding on the one that speaks most to you that day. Study it. Really take it in, the colors, the strokes, the subject matter, the execution, the essence and journal it all. Do it in great detail.

Now see if you can identify what it is about that painting that is speaking or mirroring you. It will tell you something very important about where you are right now. What you are yearning for, or what you are fearing, or something that you need to address. Analyze it! Figure it out! I guarantee when you get it, the knowing that you feel will teach you what knowing feels like! And you will have some very important information about yourself.

If you're at the museum with someone, it might be the right time now to go for tea. Share your selections and what they said to you, and why. One time as I did this exercise I found myself glued to Delacrioux's painting of Jesus in the boat. Somehow I couldn't imagine that any human could lay asleep in a boat in a huge storm such as was painted. How? I stopped. Why was I questioning this so intensely. Hmmm, did I have some real faith issues going on? I bought a postcard of the painting and kept it right in front of me, as I worked on this issue. I knew full well that it was right on. And I knew I wanted to have faith like Christ in that storm; Faith, no matter what.

One woman who did this exercise in our "Designing Your Life" group found a painting of a tiger that she loved. It had many different painting techniques positioned on different parts of the same animal, seeming to section the body into parts. It was very interesting, but when analyzed it seemed the tiger was fragmented. It gave her great knowing as she acknowledged how her life was going in so many different directions and reducing a feeling of wholeness. It was a great mirror, and she knew it, but not until the painting said it so clearly.

This exercise gives you many things: how something external can reflect your internal reality, what it feels like to KNOW your truth, and what part of you could use some contemplation and change to move you forward.

Exercise Two
Strengthening your Awareness of Knowing

This exercise is for strengthening the feeling of knowing, so you get very adept at recognizing it. The universe will also, keep you moving toward knowing constantly.

Take a sheet of paper or your journal and list times that you can remember where you truly knew something was going to happen, or who was on the phone when it rang, or someone you were going to see that day, and you knew it only by intuition. Remember how it felt when you knew you had done a good job, or clearly the opposite. Right now your greatest source for this experience is in the past, remembering the sureness of the feeling. As you journal you might mention why you were so sure, or see if you can describe the feeling. I would devote a page or more to this exercise. Whenever the feeling of knowing exists in your day, journal it as soon as possible. Soon you will recognize it easily and it will serve you tremendously.

CHAPTER THREE

Beyond Amazing

If oneness is true
And we really are connected
Then it's time we act like we're from the same womb
As though we're family.

More and more the owls became involved in intimate parts of my life. Our dance with each other was not constant, but it definitely had a flow. One late afternoon as I arrived home, I spotted a small perky owl sitting in a tree about thirty feet from the end of my driveway. It was still daylight, and I could see him straight ahead like he was a welcoming gatekeeper. Leaving my things, I slipped out of the car quietly and walked steadily toward him. He never budged. He just sat there very still and comfortably. I stopped at the edge of the woods, which was about ten feet from him. He was not disturbed in any way by my closeness.

I liked our proximity and the clear view I was getting, so I decided to stand with him as long as it lasted. I got situated in a position that felt steady and balanced and focused by looking straight into his eyes; I wanted to be as comfortable as he was. He didn't budge. He was satisfied that I was present and had no other distraction.

We stayed together in that way for what seemed like an eternity, but really it was about 20 minutes! I only mention time so you can perceive the scene. Finally, though, I grew tired. He didn't! I guess my "being" skills weren't as developed as his. So, I quietly thanked him for what I decided to call our meditation and proceeded into the house. But believe me, I was really rejoicing within myself. What was it about? Perhaps it was a simple "welcome home." Possibly he was giving me a chance to see him up close. Or maybe he wanted to make our connection more solid. To be sure I understood that we were in relationship and there were many kinds of harmony we could share.

As the happenings became more frequent I didn't become blasé. I still found myself always surprised or quite overwhelmed with the appearances and maneuvers. I was fascinated at the consistency of our relating. "Why was it happening?" I wondered. Was it that the owls perceived my openness, or my intention for life to get bigger? Did they sense how much I wanted to know more of the mystery? Or was it just the fact that I really believed in everything that was happening; that they could trust me?

I shared my owl stories with a few of my friends. Some questioned that they were real. "Perhaps coincidence?" they'd say kindly. But a few buddies were absolutely with me. My awe kept me going. I didn't want to be wrong for I felt this possibility was so powerful to life. I began anticipating their presence more often.

The last owl story that I'll share may be my most powerful, although the consistency of the owl stories has its own power. This sharing requires some history for you to appreciate. Let me go back to an earlier time in my life and a friendship that changed me. The relationship was with a man much my junior. We were sharing puzzling times in our separate lives. As our friendship grew, he was introducing me to my athletic side, a side I barely knew. We played tennis often, and he taught me to row a twin skull, a skill I adore to this day. We began to bike together and I introduced him to yoga and lots of laughter. I cherished his sensitivity. Our friendship was sweet and deep.

Roger began to yearn for children. Our relationship was not about creating family, so he began his search for a woman to share that part of life with him. We talked about it for hours. I quietly feared for the loss of him in my life, and yet so honored this biological urge, and how he was so open at sharing its reality with me.

Choices of a partner came and went, and I was always the buddy that remained, until he met Susan. Then I knew Roger was on his way. She was perfect for him, and there was even a childhood synchronicity of how they'd actually been in each other's presence at his Grandfather's cottage very early in their lives. It was all so obvious. They courted, became engaged and finally with all of us present, married with great celebration and joy.

Creating family did not happen immediately for them, but one day over a shared lunch Roger announced that they were expecting a child in April. I was so happy for them, and for me, for we all had managed to come through this journey together as family. I knew I would surely fill some role in relation to this child, and I felt great honor about that.

The nine months seemed to go quickly and in no time it was spring and close to the January delivery date. I was in touch with them to a degree, but not constantly for my life was busy with friends and work. On the afternoon of January 22nd, I had plans to go to a concert at the Academy of Music, in Philadelphia, with my sister-in-law, Jean. I was excited about the evening and decided to take a nap so I would be totally energized for the event. I laid across my bed and fell fast asleep. It was after 5:00 PM and just beginning to get dark.

Suddenly an owl hooting awakened me. It's song seemed to be right outside my window. I thought at first it was one owl, but there was a strange rakish sound with it—a sound I didn't recognize at all. I turned to look and there on a branch was a mother owl with a small baby owl beside her. It was such an amazing picture.

Stunned by this extreme presentation, I started to cry marveling at this possibility. "Your baby's beautiful," was the message I sent.

They were soon gone, and I was filled with amazement and gratitude, deep, deep gratitude. I leapt up excitedly to prepare for my evening, cherishing and feeling the depth of what had just happened. I really could hardly believe it.

The essence of that moment stayed with me through a very entertaining evening with Jean as we chatted and listened to the wonderful symphony. "Life can't get better," I thought. Little did I know.

Over dinner I shared my story with Jean. She was fascinated, but quickly moved on to other topics. Returning home and to bed, I stopped long enough to collect my late afternoon phone messages. And there it was, the message that explained the profound presentation by the mother owl that afternoon. "Hi Denny!" Roger's voice chimed, "Just wanted you to know that our baby girl arrived at 5:30 this afternoon. All is well!"

I was dumbstruck! The kingdom outside my window had announced Roger's message even before he could! This happening wasn't coming from a question that I'd asked. Was it coming out of my life, out of my relationships, out of what I was cherishing and supporting with love and gratitude? If so, this universe was more amazing and filled with wonder than I ever imagined.

None of what was happening in my life seemed to require my constant presence. What was transpiring seemed deeply embedded in the evolving of more life than just mine. And somehow I was getting it that a birth might effect everything in the universe. Richard Bach writes that there is no space, that everything is happening as one. If I contemplated this relative to Roger, Susan and my connection, and birth, it seemed to be so. But the delivery of the message has its voice also. Had Roger and I sustained something so strong that it might cause the universe to inform us of each other's goings and comings? I didn't know, but I was aware that here I was again asking a question. And because I'm asking a question there will probably be an answer someday. I'll wait, and in the meantime reverently hold how sacred my connections have become on all levels.

17

Exercise
Making a Collage

Sharing this story with you brings you and I into the realm of strengthening relationships, getting closer, being transparent, and knowing what is in each other's heart. It also, allows the knowing of yourself. Roger and I were good at both of these dynamics as we moved through so many parts of our relationship. As transformation happened the Universe chose to inform us of the depth of the connection we'd created. Working on theses connections with each other can happen in many ways. This exercise can be a great assist as life brings you together with your community and family.

When you have some extra time, gather a pile of magazines, put on some music, get some scissors and glue and find a big piece of paper. I've been known to tear open a grocery bag if I have nothing else. Casually page through your magazines and find things that you love, like you did in the museum, doing it in a relaxed way, not hurrying. Enjoying!

Cut out ads you like, scenes, sayings, pictures, colors, small details, anything that resonates with you. When you feel complete, trim the pictures down, use the glue and mount them in any configuration you choose on your "canvas." When you are finished you will find yourself fascinated with the combination because before you, is you. It's all part of you at this time in your life. And of course, there is more, for you only cut out what you saw at one sitting. Study it. See the diversity, the fun, the patterns, the essence. If someone else does it with you, appreciate each other's. See the differences and the similarities. Notice each other's choices. Ask about what you see. Place the collage in your personal space for a while, journal about it, decide what it says about you.

I did this with my 10 year old granddaughter one night and the experience was very bonding. I learned things about her I'd never known without the exercise, and the same was true for her about me. As you focus on your results, you intensify your journey, you put it out to the universe, so it can respond and support.

Exercise
Seeing Trends and New Energy in Your Life

I'm first going to tell you how this exercise came to be. My daughter invited me to see *33 Variations*, on Broadway starring Jane Fonda. It was a fabulous show, and engaged me thoroughly. I seemed to focus largely on the part the life of Beethoven played. I've been a piano student for years, and Beethoven has always been a favorite. "Moonlight Sonata," "Ode to Joy", "The Fifth Symphony" are all favorites. After the show I found myself going to Barnes & Noble, and finding CDs of great Beethoven works and playing them constantly. Not long after I went to the movies to see *The Soloist*. I witnessed Jamey Fox playing a street person who was in love with Beethoven. Beethoven was all around me. I'd turn on the radio only in that moment to hear something of his life.

I find this is how the universe designs for us. It's creating a collage that might speak to us. It brings similar repetitions to get our attention. The method of my response to this particular detail is to pay attention to Beethoven. I know I'll find the way it is relative to my life. Perhaps he and his music are healing me in some way, or taking me back to some precious time when his symphonies and concertos were like my lullabies. Maybe it is reminding me of the nourishment I get from Classical music. I may never know exactly, but I will choose to trust and focus. I respect it as a piece of the puzzle.

This exercise is for you to identify similar synergy, a coming together on your behalf. If nothing comes to you then ask if there is some focus that would nourish you. Or watch for its appearance, trusting that it will come.

When it does, and it will. Be sure to honor it by journaling.

CHAPTER FOUR

Widening the Circle

Listen, and wonder, and experiment,
Imagine, visualize, and intend,
Until all of the sudden you feel clear from within,
That the time for your leap is now.

To begin this next story I need to again give you some history. The home where I've lived with my family for years, has a mother-in-law apartment attached. It was built onto the house to allow my mother to live close to us after Dad passed on. She was such a joy, and the children loved her presence, so we knew it was a good decision. We processed the idea, looked at our space and began to design.

Mother and I were both interior designers, and this was our first collaboration. We began our design and then worked with the original builder to create a structure with a roofline I've never seen repeated. It turned out to be incredibly beautiful with lots of windows, high ceilings and a conversation nest that hung out over the back of the house. We never could decide whether a snowfall or a brilliant fall day won the beauty award from inside looking out. Mother loved it and spent eighteen wonderful years there. Then she came to a time when she needed much more assistance, so we moved her into the house with us.

This move opened up her space but not for long. Dear friends of ours were planning a move to Pennsylvania, from Los Angeles, as he was taking a teaching position at a small local college. We all had been bosom buddies for a long time, so it was a natural thing for them to decide to rent Mother's space. It was just the two of them, and they were in love with the layout along with the way the trees seemed part of the walls. The space and our relationship guaranteed that it was a great arrangement.

We had an absolutely wonderful couple of years. John was a playwright, and it was an exquisite space in which to do his writing. Our life filled up with lots of dinners together, long conversations, holidays and escapades. We grew very close.

They lived in the apartment for quite a few years until his position at the school changed. I'll never forget the day they announced to me that they were moving to Hawaii. It was something I had not expected, and I immediately felt a big loss to my life. We processed feelings, but the emptiness I was experiencing was huge. I did not want them to go. I was way out of harmony with this and saw it is as a negative predicament.

My perspective persisted until one sunny day at noon when I took my sandwich out on the patio to just relax. It was calming to feel the yard, the sun, and all the trees. But as I sat there I returned to contemplating this loss once again. How could I convince them to stay? Why was this happening? John could continue to write here and then nothing would have to change. My greatest desire was to convince them that this was not what had to be. How could I change their minds?

I sat there grieving it all as my watery eyes took in the yard. Glancing toward the creek I noticed movement in the grass at the edge of the brush. At first I didn't know what it was. I couldn't see anything, but then I perceived that it was a snake moving along quite steadily. It was great not seeing its actual body but only the brush moving, and to know it was a snake. It was quite dedicated to the edge of the yard. The other knowing that I had was that it was going to come to me!

I've never been friendly with snakes. I haven't been terrified of them as some of my friends, but we've never been in very close proximity. I had no experience of how I'd be with one close by, but I was definitely going to find out as this small reptile's movement became focused directly toward me.

It was a small garden snake, so I didn't feel the need to run. Plus I didn't feel any danger. I didn't budge. Steadily it kept coming until it was right at the side of my bare feet! As I settled into a somewhat comfortable acceptance, it slowly lifted its head and body and looked me straight in the eye. I found myself asking, "What do you want to say to me?" The small head was quick and alert as its' wire-like tongue flashed in and out. I thought that it was going to speak—and it did! "Trust the universe!" it said.

And that's *all* it said. It lowered its body, crossed over my two bare feet (might I say with tenderness!) as though it cared deeply about me, and raised itself again at the other side. It looked me straight in the eye as before, then lowered its' body and moved away. I was dumbfounded. I didn't move for a long time. Had I just imagined all this? Was it a projection of my grief?

What a message! What a messenger! Had I really had a snake move across my bare skin? I struggled to integrate it all, its meaning, its simplicity, its challenge. Clarity really did seem to surround all the words. Obviously I was being told to let go and trust. This whole shift had nothing to do with just me. It had to do with the universe rearranging itself for evolution and change, mine and theirs and who knew whom else's. It was saying to look at it as a birth.

I also, got it that I was being told to live each moment as it comes. They had not left yet, so why was I grieving? Why wasn't I trusting that we all have paths to follow, and mine was taking a turn as was my friends'.

I knew trusting this was definitely going to be a challenge. My marriage had ended, our three children were well on their way in life, and John and Kathryn had been an amazing surrogate family. The house was large, would I rent again? Would I move on? Could I trust that life would provide from its abundance as always, as long as I kept trusting? Not an easy leap forward when you're in the midst of the grief. But I heard the message, and I knew that was the challenge I was being handed.

I did have to laugh. The yard was certainly becoming my classroom, and my teachers were showing up in new forms now. How perfect was that! Yes, great abundance.

I did let go. I did trust, and it was days later that a small tree outside the house was filled with six morning doves. Each dove was snuggled on its own branch right at the place where it connects with the trunk. I knew it was another sign to understand. Well I remembered that doves symbolize prophecy, and the number six represents family. Hmmm! So, was the significance of this message that we are all family no matter where we are on the planet or the tree of life? We each have our own path, in some corner of the world and movement through time/space does not change anything as far as connections and love? The dots were connecting! And there was that message of space again! I could see that I had some healing to do. I needed to allow change. I needed to let go. I needed to trust life and know that love sustains as we move apart. Acceptance! Trust!

This lesson of letting go and trusting has been an ongoing one for me for quite awhile. I've dealt with my children moving farther and farther away, friends moving to other parts of the world, jobs changing, work with clients ending, on and on. I wanted it to become easy to let go and trust that we are all always connected. Lots of work! Lots of lessons! I needed to just keep moving along in faith and listening to my new friend, the snake. The universe would provide.

Exercise
Letting Go.

Every one of us has something to which we're attached. It could be a person, it could be a job, it could be money, it could be an expectation or an experience. These attachments are really all expectations that we're holding onto. It could be grief over someone who has passed on. You expected them to be by your side longer. You could be attached to a significant relationship that has outlived its aliveness. Sometimes it's an idea and our attachment to things staying as they are that keeps us from seeing the other side or another possibility. Attachments are usually fear based, and signify that we believe the loss will do us in, we will not be safe, life will not be as rich.

Beliefs tend to fall into this category of attachments and can really hold us back from evolving into whole beings or allowing life to transform. We do not expand to see the bigger picture.

In this exercise I am suggesting that you work on your attachments to set yourself free. I am not suggesting that things have to end, but instead that your attachment to them ending or changing is the work. To do this exercise, create a time, when you sit down and contemplate those things that you feel must stay the same. Be brutally honest with yourself, doing the entire list without judgment or remorse. Be as objective as you can. After the list is complete, choose one (one of the easiest I suggest) and make plans to detach. Let go of any outcome with that person, idea, or possibility. That's all there is to it. Sounds easy, doesn't it? It's not. Not if you do it with absolute sincerity. But the universe will support you, or perhaps remind you that this detachment just for you to experience free will, the feeling that you will be fine no matter what changes. It is necessary for life to evolve, and that reminder will assist you.

And in the meantime you must become your own witness to watching the allowing you do of all possible endings to any story, trusting all is well. Journal, hard, and long. This is blessed work!

Beliefs are the most hidden attachments. A strong belief can keep at bay amazing things that we desire; beliefs such as: "I don't deserve any thing good," "I can't possibly learn that," "when it rains it pours," and on and on. This exercise is huge work and requires digging deep into our childhood journeys something that is not done in a day! I like to suggest that you keep the list you make, doing this exercise and journaling each time you let go. And don't forget to celebrate your freedom and your willingness to grow. I wish you well.

CHAPTER FIVE

Energy in Motion

Seeing deeply what is,
Seeing how responsible you are for you,
And seeing how necessary it is

Changes your life forever.
It makes everything possible and beautiful.
Especially when you're clear.

It was an absolutely gorgeous, sunny afternoon when a phone call came and successfully pulled me away from my work. Sun, blue sky, puffy clouds, and friends can seduce me away from almost any focus, especially when it's for water sports. Experience has shown me that the result will most likely be a great adventure.

So it was my friend begging me to come out and play. I felt the excitement, and left with the sun roof opened wide, and my twin-skull fastened to the hitch. I traveled up the busy highway with a clear image of the next three hours out on the lake. I was smiling ear to ear.

Fantasizing my adventure took my thoughts far away from the manila file-folder stored on the back seat of the car. In it I had a favorite collection of magazine pictures saved for some time in the future when I might need some special inspiration for painting, color or designing a room. I remembered the folder when I heard the wind ruffle its contents and threaten to blow it all over the world. I put all concern aside remembering that nothing had ever escaped through the sun roof of my car before.

Some moments passed before I realized the paper noise was still going on in the back seat; in fact it had increased. Out of the corner of my eye I caught sight of one of the pages moving quite deliberately as if it was doing a dance. It went back and forth, back and forth as if it was alive. Spinning, it crossed the space diagonally, lifted up and took a divine dip to the floor. How curious and quite amusing, but I still did not feel compelled to retrieve the page since the car floor seemed a safe place for my collection.

Not so. My head turned just in time to witness the perfect flight of that dancing page right out of the window. I was stunned. I looked into my rear-view mirror only to see it disappearing under the wheels of trucks, smacking against fenders, and blowing in all directions. I was sure it was lost.

This drama had me totally absorbed. There weren't many torn pages in that folder, but they were all favorites, and I was so curious to know which one was involved in this "performance."

What was this about? Would the message be obvious in the subject of the picture? I had to know. Retrieving this varmit was not going to be easy. It was rush-hour traffic with everyone speeding along home, and my piece of paper in the mix of it all, seemed doomed. But I was determined! I wanted it back.

Pulling over to the side of the road, I waited patiently, poised to sprint when there was a break in the line of cars. I could see where the page had landed, and I was well aligned with its position. Suddenly my moment came. I threw the door open, raced out onto the highway, grabbed the tear sheet, and flew back behind the wheel.

My heart was literally racing. I was sure it was mutilated, but it didn't matter. I had to see what page it was. Slamming the door shut—I heaved a sigh of relief at my safety—took a deep breath, and turned the page over in my hands. I was shocked for it was a picture of a painting whose subject was a flying piece of paper. And if that wasn't enough, the entire page was completely intact, unscathed, unblemished in anyway. It was a flying piece of paper bearing a picture of a flying piece of paper! And it had flown away without harm! How strange!

For days I turned this mystery over in my mind. I would track the flow of the energy from the artist to the client, to the picture in a magazine. Perhaps I had extended the energy more by cutting it out to keep. I struggled to interpret. Was it a message to me to empty, or a message reflecting the aliveness of my moment, I was certainly flying down the highway! Was it a simple message for me to let go and fly, that I'd be safe and unharmed if I did, that my energy wanted to move and transform into something new?

The whole scene had me so engrossed, and I yearned to convey the experience to the artist, David Ligare. I tried to contact him with no luck at all. I wondered what his take would be. I knew today's catalyst, the wind, was not all that was responsible. There was something else at work.

I found myself remembering a fun conversation with a friend, Paul Midiri, years ago. We were playing with thoughts around music, about how a composition comes into existence and what happens to it. We started with the supposition that it first was a melody in someone's mind. Then if there was enough intention the melody got transferred onto paper. If the intention grew it might then be printed onto hundreds of pieces of paper, so it could be performed by many different instruments.

We truly were entertained as we thought about the piece being selected as part of a program performed by some orchestra. The conductor would arrange it for many different instruments. Parts would be assigned and learned, and the energy would transform as each musician would practice and learn their part. When the piece would finally be played with all these parts combined, the sounds would travel through space and into the ears, minds, and hearts of its listeners.

We laughed at the thought of this phenomenon. We could see the impact the listener might receive if the music penetrated his/her being, It might carry a message that the composer intended, carrying them away to some dream, or assist them in letting go, perhaps cause humming or foot tapping, or inspire something in some entirely new realm. It had the potential to resonate with their soul, or open their heart. Paul and I went on and on in our imaginings. It was a fun and intriguing preface to this flying piece of paper for it was all about energy moving and changing form.

I remembered another episode when there was a similar transfer of energy. It was at a time when I had been asked to teach a seminar as part of a conference for the American Cancer Society. I was looking forward to the opportunity for I would be attempting to help persons find ways to support their healing journey using their environment. I had some good history with this work and I yearned to do more. I prepared my talk, and gathered the notes and handouts for the class, With only one more errand left to do, I proceeded to the local dry cleaner nearby.

Driving along I pressed on the accelerator and an excruciating pain shot up my foot and through my ankle. It was awful. Pulling over I vigorously massaged my entire leg. The pain didn't leave, so I sat in my van at the curb and meditated. No luck! I gave up and decided to go to the Emergency Room. Nothing else seemed sane.

They saw me fairly quickly and after an X-ray told me that I had a sprained ankle. They outfitted me with a temporary strap-on cast and crutches and sent me home. I hobbled all the way devastated that my teaching the next day was threatened. There was no release from the pain. The first two hours back home were an intense handicapped experience. It was difficult to even get from one side of the kitchen to the other without both crutches. My foot couldn't take any weight, and I'd lost the use of both hands. Preparing food was impossible. "How do disabled people do it?" I thought. Finally I found myself fed up with my predicament.

Nothing was working. Searching my mind for guidance, I remembered a book that I'd read and adored titled, DOWN UNDER, by Marlo Morgan. In it she described a time during a "walk about" with aborigines in Australia, when she witnessed one of the natives break a bone in his lower leg. The tribe stopped everything, encircled the victim and sang until the injury was totally healed, until they literally saw the bone meld back together and the wound close. This story impacted me dramatically. Remembering it, I wondered if this possibility could be mine? I was desperate, so I vowed to make some form of healing work for me. I had no tribe, but I had me. Perhaps I could muster the same power. If they did, why couldn't I?

I went into the kitchen where I have a small couch. I snuggled into its seat, got very centered, and prayed for all the assistance I could get as I started singing. I sang and sang. I sang old hymns like, "I Walk in the Garden Alone," "Holy, Holy, Holy," and "Rock of Ages." I sang them over and over again holding tightly to my ankle and rocking back and forth. As I sang the room seemed to fill with light. I just kept singing. Slowly I began to sense that something was happening, or should I say I trusted something was happening. Tears began rolling down my cheeks as I sang out with all the passion I could muster. I truly knew what I wanted in this situation. I was clear.

I sang for at least an hour, and then I knew my ankle was healed. I put away the crutches, and loaded the car easily. I promise you that I did! The next day I taught two long workshops in high heels.

This was such a moment of awakening. When the injury first happened I went into fear and therefore a typical response to need help from the external. "What's wrong?" was my first response! Then I went to "Who do I get to fix it?" No real healing there. No experience of feeling it. It was my old behavior, my old belief system, and not what I wanted to hold as my new paradigm that the healing can come from within. The remembrance of Marlo's book was my guidance and was so sacred in helping me imitate and initiate a new experience. My singing and trusting became my tools in this experiment to manifest something new. I was processing in a different way, with a great deal of faith and confidence in me, and I was exercising what I'd come to believe. My singing had been easy and deep, and it did attract wellness very quickly. I was extremely grateful, and encouraged by the outcome.

In the following months I told this story often, to others who were experimenting in the same ways. One day I shared it in a community celebration, at Pebble Hill Interfaith Church, in Doylestown, PA. I told it almost exactly the way I've told it to you now. It was months later when a young man who had been sitting in a back row of the church that day, revealed to me how he'd witnessed a healing as he listened to the story. He said that as I spoke, an arc of energy came across the room and entered his wounded foot, an injury that he'd been dealing with for a long time. He'd had no pain since that moment. He was totally healed!

He said he was so surprised as it happened, that he was speechless. I told him I had never imagined such a possibility, that he must have been very trusting of me or aligned with my words to have received the energy so openly. That occurrence certainly helps me now as I struggle to explain this idea of how energy is always in motion, and how it has taught me that it moves from the mind to the heart, to the body, to the pen, to the camera, to pages in books, to our bodies, to photographs, to odd occurrences, to understanding, on and on. Energy lives in everything. It is all Source; all alive. And not only that, but we have access to and can direct energy at any moment.

Exercise
Raising your Vibration

The stories in this chapter hold their own illustrations of what you can do to raise your vibration and move energy. You can follow energy and observe its' changes. You can see if you are bringing your own energy up to a certain level just by feeling it or seeing it move forward into other forms of beauty, or potential, or form Just checking in to your own enthusiasm is a good way to track your vibes. If you're not feeling optimistic, positive or like life is good, start listing what you're grateful for in your life, or what needs to change.

You need to know that your hands are like two jumper cables that can pour energy into any part of your body. Living at a high vibration makes any "hands on work" more effective. In the story of my ankle, I'm sure using my hands as I sang was very helpful to my healing. Throughout this chapter are many more examples of energy transforming: the story of the man's foot healing, the movement of energy through composing, painting, singing. All of these were quite simply demonstrated through their successful outcome. My high energy in the car made a piece of paper that held the picture of a flying piece of paper . . . FLY!

It always raises our vibrations when we are doing something that is our passion and that is filling our hearts. It is our imagination and acceptance of this potential that helps us manifest. I believe it's behind spontaneous healing, amazing inventions, and really all successes of the human spirit. We can make it a commitment to keep our vibrations high.

You and I can take responsibility for "charging up" by checking in to ways our energy gets pulled down. Could be we're taking things personally, making assumptions, or judging. That's behavior that we can change if we're willing.

If we can't spot behavior that is responsible for low vibes, then perhaps we need to exercise, walk in the woods, sing, or dance to raise our vibration. There was a period of time when I was really down. I began waking up at 4:00AM in the morning for no reason. Finally I was getting a strong message to "get up and dance!" I finally began doing that and the healing was tremendous. I did it for months. I'd return to bed and fall right back to sleep.

This exercise is a big one It requires practice. It insists that you remember that you're in charge of your life and your experience. It is one you can bring into every moment, or not. You can choose to change your energy totally.

Singing was a tool in healing my ankle. Let singing heal you in some way. Sing first thing in the morning. Sing in the car. Sing when you work. Sing with others. Sing in the shower. I remember a dear friend of mine singing duets with me on the phone as he drove a long, lonely drive home from seeing a client. It was very bonding.

Choose a favorite song that you love and sing it to yourself in the mirror, smiling, looking into your eyes, noticing your posture, noticing your skin. Let the singing open up your throat and express your enthusiasm. And if singing in the mirror inhibits you, keep doing it until it doesn't!

Raising and keeping your vibration high is the most important exercise in this book because it reminds you that you are responsible for you, your happiness, your loves, your movement forward! May you become filled with high vibration and attract all you desire.

CHAPTER SIX

Journey to Safety

How clever I am with this mask
This identity that covers what's me.
My hope is that none of you wonder about
My real Truth that yearns to be freed.

My guidance began to come from so many places; not just the yard and the animal kingdom. Oh, I still heard from the owls, perhaps a deer would appear with a message, or even a tze tze fly, but I think this next story is perfect to move the picture beyond those kingdoms and into experiences that encouraged me to continue my journey within. It's a story about me and a van and a wonderful trip.

I love to drive. And I love to travel. Often my work keeps me from doing it, or I just don't take the time to plan an excursion, but I always have the yearning. I like cars and vans too. I dearly love the memory I have of a white Dodge Dart with Red leather upholstery that I owned when the kids were young. Then I moved to sports cars, and really relished a time when I got to drive a large recreation vehicle that had an amazing wheel base. I love to drive.

One day a voice on the other end of the phone said, "Remember when you asked me to call you if we needed a driver for that van from Reno? Well, the van is ready and you've got the job if you want it!" WOW! I wanted it! A dream come true. I was being given the opportunity to drive across the United States!

A "Yes," came without any thought. It was a request that was too good to be true. In the days that followed I was filled with great visions of adventure. I wondered who I would ask to join me on my jaunt, what route I would take, and who I would stop and see. I poured over maps for hours.

That call came in April and plans circled my mind until June. Very slowly, and not without intensity (!) the themes of my trip began to emerge; themes like fun, exploring new territory, experimenting, seeing new sights and visiting old friends. I laugh now for in the course of the trip, the themes changed dramatically to confrontation, forgiveness, healing, trusting, integrity and safety. During the trip, I sang a lot across America, but the stranger within me wins hands down in capturing most of the moments.

But that means nothing to you yet. Let me tell you more of the details so you understand. I'm not sure when it was that I knew I was going to take this trip alone, but from the moment I made that decision it never changed. I knew I was comfortable being alone, but being the only driver made others fear for my safety.

That fear increased as I called various friends along my proposed route for pit stop-hugging possibilities. Their responses were always the same, "Why are you doing it alone?" "Because I have to," I'd say.

Going alone was influenced mostly by my time with a friend, Jean, during my planning stages. As we sat having tea one afternoon in her living room, a sentence went through my thoughts that drained all other thought: "I feel like a total stranger to myself." The sentence was truly out of the blue. Without me saying a word, and within minutes of that internal revelation my friend got up to retrieve a book she was reading. I knew it had to do with that sentence even though I hadn't uttered a word. I obediently slipped a thumbnail into the pages knowing my guidance was coming in fast. There it was, as big as life:

> Give wine, give bread,
> Give back your heart to itself
> To the stranger who has loved you
> All your life, whom you ignored
> For another who knows you by heart
> Sit, feast on your life.

The poem was from a book by David Whyte titled, "The Heart Aroused." It contained a chapter about how in mid-life, it is time to go out and find the stranger you've left behind, the stranger that lives within. Somehow I knew I would be safe. Perhaps it was because I was so clear after reading that verse that this trip was about inner work, nothing else. It also was obvious that I was not going to be *alone!*

40

There was no tape deck in the van, but there was an every-fading radio, so I sang songs all the time. It has become a habit now of singing in the car. During the trip, songs came to my mind with messages. Songs that I didn't remember came through loud and clear.

I can't share every ecstatic moment of the trip, but one event really embodies the essence of these 3 ½ weeks of traveling in the van. I was in Lake Tahoe, and only one night into my trip. I'd found a nice campsite near a bathhouse under tall pine trees. The drive over the mountains from Reno, had been gorgeous, but I had seen all I could take in, and I was very tired. I undressed in my little van-house (!) and snuggled down for prayers and sleep. I dozed off quickly, but wakened to a feeling of intense turmoil. I wasn't afraid, instead I was resentful that I couldn't just settle in, but I just couldn't. There seemed to be demons all around me. I tried deep breathing. I listened to the night sounds. None of it worked. The chaos continued until madness seemed like the only possible outcome. In desperation I pulled out a candle and my Animal Medicine Cards, the only oracle that I'd brought with me, hoping for some clue to this plight. The card that came to me was the card of the owl! Owls again. Owl has many messages, but the message that seemed to hold resonance was "deception." I laid back desperately open to hearing its truth.

The next hour found me being confronted with every moment of deception I think I had ever lived. I was the deceiver. There was intense disappointment as I saw the faces of friends from my past, secrets, fears, anger, hatred, the deepest, darkest feelings I could possibly imagine. I tell you, I wept so deeply that I could feel cells exploding, blood massively flooding muscles, pulsations that seemed to make my eyes bulge out of my head. Finally I was desperate and reached for my journal hoping that writing would bring some peace. In my journaling I finally came to the place of knowing the deception was mostly of myself. I had deceived myself as I'd made choices, again and again that were not what we might call "high road choices." I recalled Scott Peck's book, The Liar Within. In it he spoke of how we really all are liars. I remembered how I resented that statement.

I wasn't a liar. But now I could see the lies I'd lived to protect others and myself, or to get others to love me or to get what I wanted at all costs. How deeply I had threatened my well-being. My move to living in integrity was the only safety for my soul.

After journaling pages and pages, I was exhausted, but still felt no peace. I reached for a lighter and crawled out of the van to a nearby campfire. I kneeled and prayed as I ignited my pages of writing and placed them on the ground to burn. I desperately wanted to release and knew fire was a great answer. It consumed the papers quickly as I embraced this simple ritual. I hoped it had the power to heal whatever was going on for me. I limped to the bathhouse and showered; imagining and hoping, that all the toxins were leaving my body and flowing down the drain. It was chilly, so I moved fast and tucked myself in again. Gratefully sleep came quickly, and was very deep. The next time I opened my eyes it was full daylight, a gorgeous morning.

Remembering the episode of the night before, I sat up to catch a glimpse of my "alter campfire." On the top of a grate I could see a very small piece of paper, about an inch and a half square. I literally raced to retrieve it knowing a message was there. As I held it in my hand and stared at its burned edges, tears filled my eyes. It was the only part left of all those pages. Six words covered the two sides. "Ray, so sorry, please forgive me." So, this was the last side of this issue. I needed to understand my deception and have closure with my ex-husband, who strangely enough had provided this journey. Well, I had the rest of 3 ½ weeks to write a letter to Ray, and its importance was very clear.

I think my greatest sense was how present God was. All that was happening seemed so staged. Why had it happened there at that campsite? Was it the presence of pine trees and earth? Was it the aloneness; the openness of time and space with no distractions? Whatever it was, it showed me so clearly that I was not alone and that my safety was hidden in the work I was being forced (?) to do. The next night at another campsite that small piece of paper sat on my dashboard altar. I placed a small candle next to it. Miraculously wax spilled over onto this fossil embossing it with clear wax that has preserved it to this day. It amazes me so completely. I cherish its presence tucked in my *Course In Miracles* book. You see if I had ever sat down to create that little jewel of a note, it would have been impossible. Three of the words were on the front of the scrap, and three were on the back! It was not a sentence that I had created! Whew! Artwork, by an artist messenger. My feeling of mystery, yet safety was profound. From that first night I drove thousands of miles for hours and never got drowsy. I went to the homes of friends and the tables of stranger's. I found myself stopping to help people along the way, even a young Mexican boy on the desert highway when no one else would offer him help. All he needed was a jack, and I had one tucked neatly in the back waiting for him. It was easy after that first night. I was in God's hands.

So, of course, I began to be so grateful that I'd had the wisdom and the confidence to travel alone. None of this inner journey could have come to be, if I'd had a companion, and these events were leading to safety of a different kind. It was the safety of self-transformation, faith and trust. Hmmmm, I guess my heart was changing, also.

One day after returning home, I was sitting in my car at a local intersection, when a knock came on the window. Startled, I turned to see a man cradling something in an orange piece of cloth. "I found this wounded bird," he said. "It's still got a lot of life in it. Would you drive it to the Vet near 611." I didn't hesitate. The window went down and I took the bird and placed it on the seat beside me. Tears streamed down my face as I did this job so easily. It was because I knew it was about my own wholeness. That "stranger" that was such a deep part of me and yearned for its' own truth, the one I'd masked all those years, had now joined me. This small bird so wounded but still filled with a lot of life was me. God had shown me my woundedness. And presented me with the possibility of healing. Now I would assist another with just as much care.

Exercise
Asking for Forgiveness

Throughout the course of our lives, there are things we wish we had done differently. You can certainly see from this story that it's true of me. Whether it is something we said, something we did, something we meant to do, someone we hurt, it is an innocent part of our life that now needs to be seen for what it really was, understood, so we can move from the darkness to the light. A very radical idea is to make a list of all those times and the persons involved, and make amends. It is not easy. It is not attractive. It's time consuming. The thought of forgiving brings with it many other emotions like anger, competition, fear, lust, hatred. They're all part of the lives we've lived.

Taking the time to sincerely offer the apology and the desire to be forgiven is a cleansing that beats all cleansings. Sincerity must accompany this act. Openness and honesty help too, and are part of what makes the cleansing so thorough. It will lead you toward self-love, connection, release, awareness and hope.

It is up to you to create the method of asking. It might be a letter, it might be a phone call, it might be meeting in person and being clear that you have something to say.

Some of those on our list may be deceased. It doesn't get you off the hook. If you truly believe we're all connected, it includes those who were in your life at another time and are now on the other side of the veil. A letter is a way, but Sondra Ray has a fascinating exercise where she suggests you sit quietly and picture a grid leading upwards, way upwards over your head. Then you ascend that grid in your imagination requesting the spirit of the other person to meet you there. You imagine the meeting and speak as though you were totally present to each other.

I love it, because it shows a lot of acceptance of unlimited possibility. We might as well begin that trust now. Do this exercise with great presence and deep thought. You are healing yourself on so many levels, perhaps on some levels you don't even know about.

CHAPTER SEVEN

Following The Light

O God, as we wander about
Reveal the sweet mystery
Help us see each other as kin and friend
The deer, the dove and the spider
The trees, the rivers, the stones, Family as well.

The mystery keeps pulling me forward. I feel it, wonder about it and find myself compelled. I go forward grateful for this path of discovery and testing it all the time. I press my nose to the glass of the window . . . seeing my breath in the fog and give thanks that my consequence is growth and newness. I go on and on grateful for this path of discovery.

I've mentioned Canada is a place where I go for vacation every year to connect with my family and extended family, to go deep within myself, and to experience many synchronicities. I'm there for one to two weeks in the summer. I drive up Route 81, and cross the magical 1000 Islands Bridge into "our Canada," loudly singing "Canadaaaa, Canadaaaaa. We water ski at one, and have a lot of fun . . ." Every minute my family, and friends have in that northern country has become profoundly precious. I cherish every rock and tree.

The cabin where we stay is like a mirror reflecting our changes from one year to the next. The cabin itself never changes. The mud colored broadcloth draperies, the hide-a-bed covered with a cotton bedspread, the 50's chrome and formica table and vinyl chairs (that I immediately move to the porch so I can view the lake) are always waiting. When I place my year-older self on this canvas I can almost immediately see and feel the changes in me for *nothing* or at least little has changed.

Our time there is filled with so many experiences—powerful thunderstorms, funny moments, good books, laughter, catch-up and magic. I can watch the littlest kids fishing from the dock for sunnies, or catch another nap, or line my chair up with the others facing the lake for the day's conversation and applauding each returning water skier.

One summer I was reading a book Bartholomew's, *I Come As A Brother*. It was causing a great shift in my understanding of life. Out boating in some shallow water, a shiny shell showed up on the floor of the lake. I scooped it up and it was exactly the duplication of the white silhouette on the book's cover. It had shimmered up from the bottom of the lake sand as I peered over the edge of my boat. It caught my eye and made me laugh. Another affirmation. One afternoon I was rocking to and fro in a small rowboat on the surface of the water. The hypnotic motion lulled me into a trance, and I shifted into a past life experience.

All of these happenings are supported by the open time, relaxation, and huge presence of nature. Whatever the underlying support, it all makes for a very magical time as the future and the past seem to melt away.

The water of the lake pulls me the most. One particular sunny morning I was out in a paddleboat. The water was quite still. Pushing off from the dock, I decided to put out a question. I asked to see or experience something special, without knowing what that request might bring.

I had been on the water for about an hour with no special experience occurring other than the joy of just being there with the magnificent blue sky, puffy clouds, evergreens, beautiful gray rock and sparkling water. What else could I possibly want? My eyes kept scanning the shoreline for some sighting; maybe a porcupine, or a beaver, or even a heron. No favorites, I just wanted to see the life of the lake; whatever it was that was happening behind the veil of my own consciousness. It always seemed so secret, so mysterious.

I paddled across the lake enjoying the sun. Turning around, I saw a tiny spike of a weed right at the edge of the shore. It was certainly worth ignoring. But it was funny! It looked like it was plugged into a socket. Everything around it was in shadow; and the sun was lighting it up so intentionally. Its brilliance really made me curious, especially since I'd set my request. I decided to go over and see what it was about. I moved across the water with anticipation, wondering if it was anything worth this energy . . . or absolutely nothing.

The small straggly shoot continued to glow, and when I got closer I saw that it was surrounded by lots of dead branches from fallen trees. I decided to get closer so I reached up to one of the bare branches and pulled myself forward.

The shoreline in this spot was at the base of a tall hill with huge cliffs and evergreen trees, ferns and other small plants. As I slipped under the branch I looked up to witness the sun just cresting over the ridge of the rock at the top. The sunlight streamed straight down the hill igniting everything close to the ground in its path. Its rays exposed a whole new world to me that was normally invisible. It all came into my view. There were hundreds of dewy spider webs, no thousands. They were delicately connected to bare branches, leafy branches, fronds of ferns, anything that a weaving spider could grab onto. Even the ground. Backlit by the sun I could see every strand in the network and all of the small transparent drops of dew hanging on each glowing thread. I could even see spiders.

There were large webs interfaced with small, round ones, and they were contrasted with other oblong webs. The whole scene was like a galaxy in the midst of what seemed a secret universe. To expose this universe the sun had to be right at the top of the hill, just cresting. And I had to be there just at that moment. And I was! I was stunned. Again the veil had lifted, and I had gotten my request. I stayed and stared until the sun went high, and suddenly the spotlight went out making everything disappear.

The beauty of the moment was truly amazing. There was such shimmering light bouncing and reflecting everywhere. It was a totally new visual experience for me. The fact that I had managed to arrive at that precise moment of possibility was so synchronistic and baffling. All that was required was my observation and response to a small, "lit" weed, a very *alive* escort waiting to reveal beauty and amazing joy.

For sure I cried . . . in fact just remembering it makes me cry. It was a gift. I still marvel at the timing of the sun as it opened the curtain, and at the small window of opportunity for that scene to exist. It was so exciting, my kind of excitement. I returned to camp to share my story with anyone who was willing to listen. Marie Woody, a dear friend, wanted to go and see the miracle, immediately. I knew it was gone for today, so we planned an excursion for the following morning.

Since time had everything to do with witnessing this drama, I had carefully noted that it all happened at about 9:45AM. Next morning Marie and I did it all perfectly. The paddleboat carried us and the universe cooperated. And yes, Marie wept. It's why I always shared my escapades with her. Our heartstrings seemed to be strung the same. She was right there with me.

Guidance comes in many forms, and timing is often the key. It reminds me of another time when I was traveling north on a busy highway in New York state. The day was hot and the car was overheating. My plans were to meet up with a friend at an exit about an hour ahead. I became concerned that I'd be late and Linda would leave. Trying to resolve the issue of the car overheating I lowered my speed. That way perhaps, I could continue my trip uninterrupted and arrive somewhat close to our meeting time. I kept moving forward knowing there was a reason this was happening and not having a clue what it was. Was it a gift? Perhaps that was my hope, but the reduced speed did bring the car's gauge to normal.

My travel remained uninterrupted. When I got to our meeting place, I didn't see Linda immediately and worried that we'd missed our connection. Finally, she appeared quite excited herself (this was well before cell phones.) She'd hit a massive traffic jam and couldn't get through. I got it! The universe had to slow me down to regulate our meeting successfully. Trusting, knowing, trusting, knowing; and trying not to forget to trust and know that the timing mattered! Such initiation!

Linda and I went on to our seminar happy and relieved. I chuckled at how my car was the way the universe controlled our meeting, and how I was being taught to just *trust*. The car did not overheat again. Ever! I did hope quietly within that in my future there would be a time when I didn't immediately go into a panic, but instead just smiled and knew I was being guided and protected.

Is this synchronicity happening in your life? Are you sensing moment to moment that something awaits you, that *every experience* has the potential of being a gift? Are you living in the flow? It's not easy, nor is it easy to write about. In the next story I want to share, I'm challenged again to follow the light, but now it's in the form of a remembering. It's a story about my beloved friend, Elizabeth Theodore, and her passing. Like Marie, Elizabeth was a kindred spirit and a great listener. We dialogued all the time, hashing out relationships, wonderings, and synchronicities.

A time came when we were both quite busy. Liz was the manager of a stationery store in town, and I had my design business. Because of our busyness and other distractions we began to meet less often. When finally we did get together, I noticed a change in her physical appearance but didn't connect the dots. It turned out that Elizabeth was on a new path for she had breast cancer. The disease was in its late stages, and she had been told her time was limited. She didn't talk much about it or express any fear to me. I couldn't seem to figure out whether she was comfortable with dying, or whether she just didn't want to talk about it.

Holding back had not been our usual behavior, so it caused somewhat of a rift. In the meantime she had a huge community caring for her. Friends were giving her constant love and attention, cleaning her home, shopping, cooking meals, and giving her heaps of support. Liz was one of the town comedians, so she entertained her buddies as they assisted her life.

One day as I left a doctor's appointment, I began to feel the need to see her. I drove the short distance to her house and found it filled with tons of friends. I quickly got it that Liz's time to go was at hand. I climbed the stairs to her room and found her in bed; her hospice escort on one side, her son, Adam, on the other. Everyone else was sitting in a circle on the floor or on chairs to stay close. I joined them and saw how much she was struggling against leaving. She'd fight for another breath as if it might be the one to pull her back into full life. Words of apology, love, and affection flowed back and forth between everyone. It began to sound like all one voice.

Liz had carried the dream for years of having a small cottage right on the New England coast where she could walk up and down the beach forever and watch the gulls. In a desire to help her with her struggle all her friends began calling out, "Liz, go to the beach. Go to the beach!" It became a soft, low chant of encouragement.

But it just wasn't time yet. Liz's struggle grew. I wondered how long it would last, whether it would get worse, whether any help would come. I tried to stay open, but it was very difficult.

Suddenly in my mind I was remembering another time when I stood in a circle with an artist by the name of Remo Saraceni. He was demonstrating a phenomenon of how energy moves from one person to another when they touch. He used a small ball, which he explained was wired. Two participants held the ball and then we all joined hands. The ball sent out a loud buzz as we connected. When one person in the circle disconnected the buzz ceased.

The fact that I was remembering it in this moment made me suspect that it might be the help Liz needed for her transformation, but I was clueless how. I considered it carefully. What was the message? I wondered whether it was actually energy that was going to help Liz leave. Would it give her assistance if we joined hands? It was hard to believe or trust that this memory I was experiencing was inspired guidance, and even harder to feel appropriate making the suggestion in this quiet setting with everyone so intensely focused.

I felt very timid. I had not been a witness to someone dying before, so I was in my own personal struggle, but the urge did not go away. Humbly I suggested to the circle that perhaps, if we all joined hands with each other, including Liz we could help the transition. Very gently a tired but committed group reached out to each other.

There was a huge sigh, a sound of letting go, and our dear friend moved on with peace and grace. A powerful feeling of gratitude and relief immediately filled the room. All of us were so happy for her. I could feel Liz's energy hovering above us. Returning to the room later I felt very connected and complete.

My drive home seemed longer than usual. I thought I would be crying, but instead I was filled with that same peace and a feeling of Divine accompaniment. When I got home the phone rang. It was my son, Carl, who was very aware of my relationship with Liz. It gave me the opportunity to share some more. We ended our call, and a few hours later I found the following piece in my e mail.

Now she sways with the field of wheat we call the Universe
Knowing all, loving all, embraced and embracing all that is.

The space that was there yesterday, filled with her,

Is now a void in this level of existence.

Our conscience can no longer think of her as there.
Our thoughts can make no more of her than a memory or an
imagined figure.

For she is truly gone from us.
We cannot learn from, laugh with or look at her again.

And now the place we call heaven
Which she called the universe unlimited by mortal being,
Shifts to allow another energy into its pond.
The ripples from the introduction of that new energy cascade
Across eternity and through all that is and can be.
Like a scent that mixes evenly with the air of environment,
So does she.
But with the shudder of her transition, the Universe
Trembles with new strength.
The energy available grows as galaxies and light react to
The new formula for existence created by her transition.

And when the surface of the pond begins to settle back to its
placid being,
The walls shudder for less than a moment,
And eternity expresses its entity in another
Symbol of life in our plane.

CARL DAIKELER

How powerful that this poem had come through my son. Its
beauty and depth was electric and created a profound concept of

the phenomenon of death. With Carl's permission we printed it on the program that was handed out at the Memorial Service for Liz.

At the end of our phone conversation, Carl had suggested that he and I agree on some sign that we'd send to the other upon passing. It was a fun and courageous sharing for it's not easy to talk about these things especially between a parent and a child. Carl decided that if he died before me he'd send me a red ribbon in the mouth of a white dove. As he said this my eyes went across the room to a piece of red ribbon hanging out of my gift wrapping drawer. I promise! He could hardly believe it when I told him, and neither could I.

Days after, as I drove along in my car, a raven, Liz's favorite bird, flew dangerously close to my windshield carrying a red piece of trash in its mouth! I roared and knew that my funny, wonderful friend's blasphemous humor was still alive and well, and so was her Spirit.

I'm reminded of a word that Depak Chopra coined: synchrodestiny. It's definition is that the synchronicities in our lives create our destiny. What occurs to me is how much synchronicities deepen my understanding of the vastness of life, which certainly has to change my choices and therefore my destiny.

Exercise . . . Be in Nature

This is the best exercise of all! Spend time outside alone! Angelus Arrien, a spiritual writer and shaman, suggests that everyone spend one hour outside a day, no matter what the weather! Do anything, lay on the ground, identify trees, plant flowers, hike, commute on foot or by bike. Be outside! Experience the seasons, smelling all of them, feeling the crunch of the leaves, the crispness or the silence of snow, the softness of grass. Sit on the bank of a river or a creek. Watch for signs. See everything that is happening around you. Notice all the different colors in the bark of a tree, what direction the creek is flowing, where the roots enter the ground. Be mindful. Know the planet on which you create your life. Be as intimate with it as you are with your own body.

Exercise
Embracing your Darkness

Not only is it important to follow the light wherever it is and wherever it takes us; it's as important to recognize the darkness, especially our own. There are times or situations when the darkness wins in our behavior, which leads to guilt for the unenlightened choices we've made.

The time comes when we need to revisit those times with courage, compassion and understanding. The reality is when we were making our choice, we did not have the depth of understanding that we have now. As understanding creeps in, and creeping in is just what it does, we begin to look into the past and wish, yearn, cry to ourselves that we could have done it better. This awareness is precious. It reflects our growth and new understanding. And it gives us the opportunity to SEE and to forgive ourselves.

Here is what I suggest as your exercise. Being as present as you can to those times, choose a way you want to move through them with your heart. It may be a ritual, it may be journaling, it may be prayer, it could even be dance or role playing. Hold close to your heart the ways you wish you had chosen better. You may cry. Crying is very cleansing. You may hurt. Honor the pain, cherishing that you know what it's about.

Lastly hold yourself. It was the past. You are growing and evolving, but you, yes you specifically, had to be where you were then to get to now. Embrace the journey and choice you made as dark and part of your innocence at the time. Hold lovingly within you those who were involved. Hold it for as long as you need. And hold yourself. Feel yourself as deeply inside as you can, and be willing, when you're ready, to forgive yourself, knowing you'll move forward into new choices.

Be grateful for forgiveness and the chance for new possibilities. Know that forgiveness is part of Truth, and rest in the powerful healing of this exercise. Be willing to sacredly let the darkness slide away. Imagine it happening. See it as a river or a vibration that is going away and is immediately replaced with light as efficiently as flipping on a light switch in a dark room.

Will this guarantee no darkness is left? No! But in this present moment all you need to celebrate is your willingness and the possibility of forgiveness being complete. You have healed yourself profoundly.

This exercise insisted on being at this place in the book. If it doesn't work for you now, bookmark it and know that when you do need it, perhaps at a very hard moment, you can come back to these words and heal.

CHAPTER EIGHT

Challenging Beliefs

The Unknown may be the place
From which we ought always begin.

I think it's an innocent place
Without expectation or lack.

I've told you that I've come to believe we are all on a spiritual path, and that there are guides that we cannot see, and they sometimes come in the form of winged creatures or car gauges. And I've shared how I've encouraged myself to open to these beliefs so I can move along faster and enjoy the revelations more. In this chapter you will see that I was truly challenged as a fascinating chapter began to unravel and made me question whether I could go out on this particular limb. Things got really fuzzy.

But first let me say that *all* of these experiences have been very confronting for me. When they've happened, I've been standing knee deep in old beliefs and paradigms. The occurrences were dramatic and couldn't help but get my attention. I guess with me the universe has needed to bring on the drama so I could see my limited thinking! I am so grateful! It has given me a chance to see that life is much bigger than I imagined, and that I can live with much more knowing and possibility.

The title of this chapter might better read *Challenging My Beliefs* for these experiences have demanded big shifts in me. From moment one I've been saying WHAT? I kept saying it because everything that was crossing my line of belief was something I didn't expect. I can also, say that none of the stories in this particular chapter were asked for. They just showed up!

The first story happened many years ago when my husband, Ray, and I were still creating a life together. We took a biking tour through Holland. The trip was a gift from him and had the promise of 10 days of utter bliss. We began with a stop in Amsterdam, and then met the biking group in Lisse, proceeding to pedal our way around Holland.

It was April, so we were present for the spring flowers, just fields and fields of them. Holland at tulip time! Oh my! Tulips and hyacinths were everywhere, deep with colors and scents. I will tell you that biking past a field of purple hyacinth is something you might never forget. It actually makes you feel drugged. You know yourself that one hyacinth is an amazing experience of your nose. A field of them produces the biggest aromatic experience I've ever had. Wow!

The tour was really wonderful with a string of days biking past cows, canals, houses with thatched roofs, and outdoor cafes. We spent each night at a different inn. Each time was a big celebration because we'd made it, we'd peddled many miles. My body was feeling depleted as I neared the end of the 10 days, but I was in amazing bliss.

The last town on our tour was Lisse, where they were holding the national Tulip Festival. We arrived mid-afternoon and went straight to a park in the middle of town. It was beautifully manicured with huge trees, green grass and one garden after another. I sat, or I should say collapsed, on a lawn at the end of rows of yellow and red tulips with hardly any spine of my own to hold me upright. The flowers were standing taller than I.

I had seen so many tulips by now, so many that I really felt an intimacy with them. Add to that my intense tired, and you'll know that I was in an extreme state of vulnerability. All my defenses were down, and I could feel only the moment. Being in this extreme place often creates a window where the universe can play, and so it did.

Sitting there my glance lowered to a tulip standing just under my nose. It was yellow and seemed to have a face; a face that was lifted up to mine with great presence. Feeling as though I was going to fall into it, I found myself speaking to this face. "What are you doing here?" I asked. "Why are you here? What is your purpose?"

There was no lapse of time where I could question what in the world I had slipped into, what sanity I had lost, for this flower answered me gently and quite directly. "Do you see that group of people walking toward us?"

I raised my glance and did indeed see an approaching group of visitors to the park. "I am here to be beautiful for them!" she said.

A flower was speaking to me telepathically! Now that means that I wasn't literally hearing a voice, but I was hearing its message through thought forms within my head. I could have assumed it was just me thinking. But I knew better.

I felt awed by the simplicity of this flower-being's answer. It's clarity of intention. It's message said that it was important in the midst of such a multitude of tulips like itself. Being beautiful was its primary purpose. Hmmm.

Besides that this tulip spoke to me! I could no longer think of flowers as inanimate or mindless. I could no longer hold to any fact like . . . they live without intelligence or intention. Another belief shattered.

This event was really precious to me. I love flowers. Considering them live companions made them even bigger blessings even though it was hard to believe. I knew I would study them more and try to understand. I knew all my walks in nature would change dramatically. I would now feel honor in the presence of every tree and every plant, even a weed at the edge of a lake that doesn't speak but only (only?) glows. This world of aliveness and connection had spread from owls and snakes to flowers and trees and they probably all had the ability to speak to me, to all of us.

The Truth is what we're all wanting. These lessons that I was getting of "real reality" amazed me, and definitely contrasted to the way I thought things were. These discoveries showed me how my beliefs in the past have kept me in a diminished sense of life and controlled what would happen to me on a daily basis. Even my joy was limited because I wasn't seeing how big the picture really is. Perhaps you and I are only beginning these lessons for I sense many more beliefs will be shattered as we move along our path.

And so my initiation continues. I keep experiencing new truths, and I'm challenged to *use* what I see; and to live it all. An opportunity to live in an altered way came not long after my return home from Holland, when my son David called. He was traveling with a group called *Up With People*. His location at that moment in time was California (I was in Pennsylvania.) When he called he was very difficult to hear. He seemed very upset. I asked him to slow down and be clear, so that I could understand what he was saying.

He proceeded to deliver an intense message with great gulps and tears. "I've hurt my back terribly. I don't know what to do. The chiropractor, who is hosting me has said I'll never dance again, that I need a back brace and surgery. I don't know what to do, Mom! I'm terrified."

There were 3000 miles between us and I was terrified too! My son, was definitely in pain, and I was a mother who had been getting a lot of guidance on a lot of levels. But right now I was a typical mother in an emotional relationship with extreme trauma, and therefore knowing and wisdom weren't easy to come by. Truths don't just roll off your tongue at those times. I found myself typical in wanting to reduce his pain, have the right answer. Plus I was scared myself. I was feeling very human and ATTACHED!

Allowing this to happen can totally shut down your intuition, so it is important to struggle as best you possibly can, to move into a softer, more trusting place. I began to pray. I didn't know what else to do. I asked for words for this young man, who was sitting on the edge of a life disaster and whom I loved deeply. He needed guidance, and I had to rise above my frustration and pain. We both knew this moment could change his life forever. And so I prayed hard. "Lord, give me words, for I have none to fill this soul or to shift this energy. I'm so scared that I'll answer wrong."

In seconds the words came . . . "Is that what you believe?" I said to him as I gulped.

I heard him gulp too and go silent. I was even shaking at my words. "What?" he asked, as if he hadn't heard me.

I took a deep breath and repeated, "Is that what you believe is now the truth for you?"

Well, of course, it wasn't the truth he wanted. But being asked whether it was the truth he believed was a strange question, especially when the question came from his mother. A trained Chiropractor had told him these facts. Could he, a 19 year old, question an authority's words? "I don't know." he stuttered.

"If you believe it David, then perhaps that is what will be," I found myself saying. "I guess you'll need to decide whether you believe it or not. In the meantime I'll call your chiropractor here and ask his advice. You say you're wearing a brace? I'll tell him. I also, know a healer near your location. I will call him too. Pray David, and I love you, darling."

I had successfully come into the moment and trusted what came to me. And I was trusting myself.

"Thanks, Mom." He said. His tone was different. There was less fear. My shaking had subsided a little.

I called our chiropractor here in the east and shared everything. As I suspected, he was appalled at this drastic diagnosis. He asked me to tell David to remove the brace immediately, and that he would see him the minute he returned to give him exercises for the injury." You see when I described the problem, it turned out that the situation was identical to what our chiropractor had experienced with his back. (the universe at work again!) He was very familiar with this kind of situation, and could easily advise him! David returned within a week for some time off. Dr. Bill saw him right away.

I want you to know the happy ending, so you can cherish and trust the message of this story. David chose to trust my words that day. And now at this writing, he is 40. He sings, dances, lifts heavy objects, and lives without back pain (unless he forgets to stretch and honor his back.) Amazing? I think so except that I'm getting that it isn't amazing. It's what we choose to believe that creates our reality. Nobody can predict our destiny. We may have problems and situations to face, but if we believe that we have the power to move through everything with gratitude and trust, nothing will be a life disaster, everything will be an *alive* moment or, if you will, a *gift*. This is huge, and really quite simple. So believing may just be the answer to so much in life.

My next tale is also around beliefs, beliefs that I truly did not hold as possible. To let you know where I was before this story began, I had lost my mother after many years of caring for her. Her passing was not a surprise nor was it very painful for I felt she had left her body many years before and her physical parting was a blessing for her. Her quality of life had changed drastically, and she was barely present. I really trusted that she wanted to leave.

Her passing was peaceful, and I had some significant signs from her after she left that were quite typical. I knew she was in a good place, and I didn't expect or believe in any continuation of our relationship in any form.

Mother had been gone for about three years, when I decided to attend a conference of American Society of Interior Designers, in Florida. My decision to go was late so I knew plane arrangements might be problematic. I called for tickets and was told that I'd be routed through Chicago. I was amused to be flying west to go south, an entirely different direction, but I took the reservation and was issued a ticket. It occurred to me that since I was living this amazing life of lessons and synchronicities, this might be another adventure. I was getting good at sensing these times.

As I packed and prepared for the trip I noticed a small paper-mache lion that my mother had made. For absolutely no explainable reason I felt an urge to put it into my bag and place it on the dresser in my hotel room. This was something that would normally not occur to me, but I followed the cue.

My plane ticket was for the 17th of August, the day before my birthday. It was a beautiful day as I drove to the airport, went on to the gate and took a seat. There was a long line of people checking in, so I suspected the plane would be full. My eyes lit on one particular woman, and I suddenly *knew* she was going to be my seat partner. Hmmm, I'd never had an intuition like that before, unless we go back to the owl in the brush.

We boarded the plane and sure enough, my hunch came true as the woman moved straight toward me and took the seat. I was quite excited about such an obvious knowing, and wondered at the reason it had happened. When she was settled, I shared the story of my intuition. She loved it and seemed to have no problem with my sureness. We laughed and enjoyed fun conversation all the way to Chicago. That was her destination so we said good-by. I wondered again, why I was routed through Chicago.

It didn't take long to find out for down the aisle came a woman headed straight toward me. She had lots of stuff with her, and we were both amused with the length of time it took her to "fix" her spot. She was very friendly, and I looked forward to our trip.

Once she was settled we moved into very easy conversation. She'd read the book I had on my lap, and it was one of many books we'd both read and loved. Our similar interests kept us well engaged. I asked her if she lived in Chicago. "Not yet," was her answer. "My husband and I are moving there soon, so I was setting up bank accounts and post office boxes."

That prompted me to share that I had a friend on television in the windy city. "Oh," is it Janet Davies?" she asked.

I was stunned. "Do you know her?"

"Very well, she said. Her husband grew up on our block and was very close to us. I attended Janet and Steve's wedding.

Well, I knew I was hot on a trail here. "Oh my goodness what a coincidence," I said, "My husband and I were invited also. We just couldn't attend." The synchronicities were coming so fast that it made us both perk up to the conversation.

"So, why are you going to Florida?" I asked.

"Oh, my daughter in law is giving birth tomorrow. She's being induced."

"Really!" I said. "Hmmm, nice. Tomorrow is my birthday." Huge sensations were pouring through me. I could feel that I was on a path of no return. I timidly asked, "Do you know if it's a girl or a boy"

"Oh yes!" She said. It's a girl.

"And her name." I said, as I bit my tongue.

"Hannah," she chimed.

My head was spinning. My mother's name had been Johanna. My birthday was tomorrow. Why had I met this woman? Was this what "going through Chicago," was about? This woman and I had connected like soul-sisters from the moment she finally got her bottles of water tucked into the seat pocket. I wanted to stifle myself, but I knew I was committed. I couldn't stop the flow. Every cell in my body was screaming what I didn't want to face. Was my mother's spirit being birthed into the family of this woman, tomorrow, on my birthday. Had I lost all reason?" "Just forget it," I thought. "Just shut up and read your book. You've gone too far."

Well, what I'm sure you now are beginning to understand, is that when the universe has been this successful at getting your attention, and you're having this much fun, you can't turn back! And so . . . .

I turned to my seat partner, and said something I hardly believed myself, "Your children are birthing my Mother's Spirit!" and proceeded to explain why I thought so.

"I know." She said. Well, if you think we were connected before, we were now glued to each other. "What in the world was going on."

My love of birth, and babies, and especially mystery enlivened my imagination. I found myself groping for the ways I wanted to live this, how I could assure that I remained in the middle of as much of this birth event as was appropriate. I told her I really wanted to hold the baby. She agreed that it was not only possible, but important. Our plans were laid.

We decided we'd begin right away when we landed by her getting her rental car and driving me to my hotel. She promised she would call me the next day when the birth was complete. My head spun and spun, but I also will tell you that I was in bliss. This was truly an adventure that I couldn't have fathomed, and was challenged to accept. All of that made it so delectable.

When I got to the hotel I was very high and began to unpack. I was loving my room, loving being away, and wanted to really live this experience. Opening the suitcase I found mother's small lion that I had so innocently thrown in at the last minute. Smiling, I placed it on the dresser totally understanding it's presence and my initial impulse to put it in my bag. It had belonged to her. Tomorrow was August 18th, the sign of Leo. Mother was going to be a Lion like me. It was perfect that I was led to bring it along.

Signs kept happening. I decided to go to the gym before swimming, so I dressed in shorts with my bathing suit underneath. As I walked the treadmill, Johnny Mathis, mother's favorite singer, sang out a song on the wall hung TV. As I finished and settled onto a chaise in the outside pool area "Born Again!" blasted from the speakers, louder than all the other music that had played! The universe didn't want me to doubt for a minute.

The next day at noon I lost my patience and dialed the family. Four rings brought me to an answering machine. I stood frozen in disbelief as a young girl's voice announced. "Hi, this is Carley. We're not here right now, but leave us a number and we'll call you back!"

I hung up and broke into laughter. My father's name was Carl. What did that mean? Were Carl and Johanna now going to be sisters? It actually seemed possible. Names seemed to be leading the way.

A return call came around four, and I was told that Hannah had arrived. Her delivery time was 3:26. That time was significant for Mother's birth date had been March 28th, 3/28. I was breathless.

I need to hesitate for a moment and tell you that the fact that the birth time was two minutes off could have killed my belief, but I had too many signs running, and too much knowing going on. You have to pay attention to the details, and then decide what you choose to believe. Acceptance may be tested.

I was fascinated and a believer! We set a time for me to come to the house, and she told her family very simply that I was a woman she'd met on the plane. She shared that it was my birthday also, and I thought it would be fun to hold the newborn. They were very open to my visit.

I went through my next day's events at the conference and prepared for my extracurricular fun. Great excitement was running through me as well as the question, "Is any of this true or real? My new friend picked me up, and I shared all of the new details. She loved it all. I shared how I wondered if this infant might be filled with some of the power and strength that had lived in my mother, how I was extremely curious about this new granddaughter/daughter of theirs.

But none of the above matches those amazing moments when I sat with those two women, holding a beautiful, healthy, baby. The three of us sat close as I held the fourth entity, Hannah. She was so tiny, so easy to hold, very healthy, very peaceful. She had those exquisite hands that we all marvel about in newborns, the tiny, delicate, fingernails. I looked at her gentle face and the gentle, soft faces of the two other women as I witnessed my own deep gentleness and my awe at this new appearance of my wonderful mother's soul being born again. I wept deep inwardly for the sacredness of the Divine Birth and at the same time knew that this moment was quite ordinary. It's happening all the time.

At this present moment we were a daughter, a mother, a grandmother, and me, another daughter/a new friend. And if all that was true, each one of us including Hannah, had previously been a daughter, a mother, a mother-in-law a grandmother in a different sequence. We were all four present in this moment together, and now there was a suspicion that we'd been in some or all of those roles before, somewhere, sometime, on some level. At least I was confronted with my having been the daughter of this new being who was moving into being a daughter and granddaughter in a new family in Florida. How could I not believe in oneness with all this Divine patterning? I was seeing it play out so literally in this physical reality, as we all sat there related to each other in some way. I felt it in my bones. It felt good. All of us on the planet, you and me and all, are constantly changing places as each other's sister, brother, daughter, mother, father, grandchild, friend. We've been in each role probably thousands of times with each other. We ought to be treating each other with such care. You and I are each other's kin.

Two months later I heard from this friend again when she called to ask if I would meet her in New York, on October 8th. She was coming in to visit her daughter who lived in Brooklyn. I laughed again for moments earlier I'd had a client call and cancel for that exact date. My answer was, "I'd love to."

You'll stay with me at my daughter's?" She said.

That would be lovely," I said. "What's your daughter's name?"

"Jillian." She said.

I closed the manuscript I had been reading when she called. The cover page smiled up at me. *Jillian's Journey!* Names had been the primary signs.

I've had many wonderful times with Hannah and her family. And I just keep learning to open so I can witness and believe the unbelievable!

Exercise
Trusting and being open

The practice of this exercise will be ongoing. You've witnessed me in this state throughout this book. That doesn't mean it is not challenging every time.

Your first job is to simplify your life somewhat, for these synchronicities will have no place to enter if you're always booked. Secondly, it means you have to give up control. If I was bound and determined to go directly to Florida, instead of through Chicago, I would have foiled the universe. Third, open up your thinking to acceptance, accepting the impossible, listening carefully so you're hearing the details and can connect the dots. Give up texting, or always being on the internet so you have open time to flow and be present in the moment. This is how the universe can and will connect with you.

I'm sure this is all happening to me *because* I have so much to learn. But I also, think it is happening, because I am very accepting and very willing! Stay open! Consider the absurd. Be courageous and admit your fears, your questions and what you do accept! Do it over and over again! You'll get really good at knowing what deserves your sacred attention! Practice until it is truly a piece of cake.

CHAPTER NINE

Squirrels and Cats, Oh My!

Your Holiness reverses all the laws of the world.
It is beyond every
Restriction of time, space, and distance,
And limits of any kind.

THE COURSE IN MIRACLES

And so my paradigm continues to shift. As I am presented with new possibilities everyday, I become more conscious. Now I need to learn how to be true to this new consciousness. I attempt to align what is shown to me with my present beliefs and see what it all looks and feels like. I try to understand how these beliefs apply daily.

I've shared how these stories have challenged me. And how therefore my paradigm is shifting with great regularity. I seem to keep moving through one door after another, each one presenting new ways of thinking, new realities, and new possibilities. Each event that has happened has seemed like coincidence, but has in fact been in direct alignment with my life and my thoughts; an important new connection. And through all of these experiences, I have been changing, becoming more open and holding life on the planet and life after with much more trust and understanding (and should I say awe!). I find myself getting much more comfortable with the idea that nothing is confined to the usual logic we think governs our lives.

Animal by animal, friend by friend, happening by happening I move along. This next story moved me forward yet again and seemed to happen by chance. It is a simple story that involves squirrels and happened one evening when I was driving to meet a friend for dinner in the nearby town of Doylestown. I was late for our meeting, so I drove quickly through all the familiar back roads to avoid the rush-hour traffic.

A squirrel suddenly dashed across the road in front of me. I saw it much too late, and even though I jammed on my brakes I hit the helpless victim. I hadn't wanted that to happen, so I was upset, but keeping my agenda as a priority, I didn't stop. I hurried on uttering apologies under my breath and ignoring the sinking feeling in my stomach.

Jayson, and I met and walked the three blocks into town looking for a delicious meal in one of the local restaurants. It was a warm and balmy evening filled with great visuals of town lights and quaint shops, along with the precious sounds of spring. Jayson and I talk easily, so our conversation was immediately full and stimulating. Enjoying it all, I became aware of a squirrel on a low branch in a nearby tree we were passing. He was about shoulder level to me screeching non-stop with a bushy tail standing straight out behind. The racket was wild, as he seemed intent with harassing me.

Suddenly that feeling of intense "knowing" that I keep talking about was with me again, a feeling that is often followed by an affirmation that "It's true." I knew this squirrel was focused on me personally. In truth I sensed that he/she was admonishing me for my carelessness during my drive. I was stunned. Hitting that squirrel had been an accident and had happened miles away and at least a half an hour before.

What began to creep into my thoughts was how this harangue from this agitated messenger was most likely coming out of a bigger reality. Even though the encounter between my car and the squirrel took place five miles south and a half hour earlier in Warrington, no time and no space was blocking any awareness of the incident in Doylestown. The "squirrel kingdom" knew about it and was not happy. This messenger was informing me that a squirrel's life matters, and if I didn't think so I was incorrect and highly disrespectful.

The possibility that this small animal on this branch was delving into deep reality with me and trying to show me that there was a consciousness that pervades that has nothing to do with distance or space. This was strikingly amusing and challenging. I'd read Richard Bach's book, No Space, No Time, but those were words on paper. It seemed that I was being educated through a very common occurrence that happens all over our roads day after day. For a split second I laughed inwardly imagining I was part of a Disney film with all the animals, following along behind me, falling into holes, climbing up trees, chattering away. But I wasn't in a Disney film, I was walking down the streets of Doylestown, and this whole scenario defied logic.

I could hardly keep walking let alone talking. I didn't tell Jayson what was happening. It was too big yet for my mind to hold, and would have sounded silly. What would I have said, "This squirrel is scolding me because I ran over one of its species on my drive here!" I wanted to preserve a bit of the sanity Jayson still trusted I had. But I was feeling like I'd pressed the button in an elevator and suddenly ended up with the elevator leaving the building and traveling into another reality. When the door finally opened there were no walls and ceiling, and. I wasn't quite sure where to step or who I was.

I was well aware of all the times I've been careless with animals on the road, or just totally oblivious, but in today's world where wildlife is scattered in amongst neighborhoods and highways it happens all the time. When it happened before to me I was always sorry. And I would certainly always brake for animals when the timing was right. I could see the disconnect of my human consciousness in relation to the real Truth. I could see how this other kingdom expects and wants more in their relationship with humans on the planet. A multitude of possibilities and messages were forcing a shift in my whole being about all that is. And my "proof" was a squirrel hanging on a branch exactly at my right shoulder and screeching in my ear. It wouldn't let me dismiss it.

I found it difficult to remain totally present with Jayson. I really needed to be home on the couch with my cat Bonnie, letting it all sink in. The phrases, "All life is sacred" and "We are all one" took on a new resonance. Squirrels had upped my respect for them big time!

Bonnie was another one of my teachers from the animal kingdom. She had lived with me for about 19 years. This story about her and about us is also simple and created huge impact on my thinking. I got Bonnie when my son Carl, brought her home from college. Soon, of course, she became mine (a very typical occurrence between sons and mothers!) I cherished Bonnie, and we had a pretty normal cat/ mistress relationship, but as time went on that changed.

She was an indoor/outdoor cat, and did some pretty profound mousing, which pleased me most definitely. One year, though, her mousing was off as was evident by the obvious mouse droppings in the kitchen. That was early December. The family mentioned the omission to Bonnie, and she responded in time by depositing a mouse under the Christmas tree in full view of all. We were delighted and laughed heartily over her "gift" thanking her profusely.

Her prowess and responsibility grew through the rest of the mouse season, but what was more sacred was my learning about how easily Bonnie could understand what I wanted. This kept happening with pretty ordinary conversation from me, and some responsive cat sounds from Bonnie.

As Bonnie and my relationship became more fluid, I felt I was bringing "my classroom" from the back yard into the four walls of my home. Our life together was long and fun. She, like all cats, loved the sun and hunting. I adored watching her outside when she'd stare at brush for hours waiting for some four legged to stir and let her know its presence. I envied her patience and adored

81

how alive she was in all that stillness. Often I'd sit down to a meal and find Bonnie in the empty seat across from me looking quite ready to share a meal or have a conversation.

Years of relationship went happily by. Bonnie's hair began to thin, but she still seemed quite healthy until one day when I couldn't find her. It took awhile to discover that she was nesting under a skirted table in my bedroom. She seemed ill, so I knew she wanted privacy. I comforted her and went on with my day. A few mornings later I entered my bedroom to find a squirrel outside the window doing that same kind of scolding and racket that had occurred before. It was perched on the deck rail just opposite the table and was clearly telling me that Bonnie needed more than privacy and I'd better get to it.

Embarrassed I gathered Bonnie up and took her off to the vet. The prognosis was not good. There was surgery that I could do, there were pills for her thyroid, but as we sat there with our ability to communicate, Bonnie very clearly let me know that she didn't want any part of *any* of it. She was ready to leave and very comfortable about it. Her eyelids lowered slightly and she bowed her head to indicate that all was well and she expected me to move forward with her desires.

When the vet returned, I shared our decision. He seemed totally at peace with our choice and excused himself to allow Bonnie and I time to put meaningful closure on our journey together. She was lying with her back to me about three feet away. I soulfully watched her struggle up onto all fours, turn her body around and come over to me. Crouching down a bit, she reached out her paw, and gently placed it directly on my heart. I don't have the words for you, but I can tell you I was right back to feeling like I was stepping out of that elevator and seeing/feeling only sky and clouds and angels. I didn't know Bonnie and I could get that close. She had to show me.

When Bonnie was complete, she withdrew her paw, turned and went back to her original spot. I found myself whispering to her between my tears, telling her how much she meant to me and how much I would miss her, thanking her for the life she'd shared. Her expression was reforming me, shaping me the way that love does. I quietly left her there to continue her journey and drove home crying softly and deeply. I felt in the midst of amazing grace.

Her leaving made the house feel quite empty, but not for long. I don't mean to imply that I quickly went out and got a new pet. Instead what occurred was quite unusual. When I came downstairs a few mornings later, I passed the laundry room door where I found five walnuts very carefully placed in an arc on the floor. They were set quite perfectly, each with the same amount of space between. They reminded me of the arc of a rainbow, or the arc of some invisible energy?

I was about to pick them up, but somehow I felt reluctant to disturb the picture. Instead I tried to make sense of it. There had been no one in the house but me. There was an open basket of walnuts in the living room, and I wondered if a squirrel had gotten into the house. There were no signs that suggested such a thing. And those walnuts were just placed too perfectly. Suddenly a feeling of knowing returned, the feeling that there was going to be something revealed, the feeling that I was again in the zone of learning. Was the veil thinning? It reminded me of a piece in *I Remember Union,* by Flo Aeveia Magdalena

"Here was a knowing, a recognition, a feeling of protection and sanction. Hallow and sacred, it called to me. It was a place of wisdom-a window through time to the dimension of spirit-where the veil was thin and the magic near."

I left the walnuts there in their simple configuration. I needed to pass by them more and keep visiting their perfection and their message of the unknown beyond the rainbow.

The next day there were more walnuts. I found three in the dining room placed just as carefully, one leaning against a table leg and two against two chair legs. They weren't askew at all in fact they looked the way they would look on a canvas if an artist had carefully painted them in that position.

My reasoning kept trying to take over by telling me that this was nothing. But it also was not explainable. There had been no visitors in the house. I struggled with what was happening. Just when I thought I had come up with a reasonable explanation a walnut appeared squarely "placed" in the middle of a throw rug in the kitchen (again, a picture of perfect composition), and the following day another showed up leaning against a leg of the living room coffee table.

I tell you this growing display of walnuts had me stunned. There was no reasonable theory, and I even began to feel uncomfortable.

The consistency and placement defied all reason. Finally I allowed the possibility that it might be Bonnie. Nothing else made sense (even though I smirked at the insinuation). Was Bonnie communicating with me that things are different than the way I see them just as that squirrel in Doylestown; that I need to get my mind out of the way so I can know that things aren't nearly as limited as I believe, and In fact they're quite amazing?

I began to love the possibility that it might be Bonnie continuing to play and communicate with me. I then considered that squirrels were responsible, moving walnuts around as a message that there was a far higher and more playful road with the animal kingdom than the one I'd driven down with careless abandon.

Before I finally collected the walnuts I counted them. There were eleven the number of mastery. If my deductions were correct, Bonnie and the squirrels were certainly demonstrating mastery. Finally weeks later I found one more walnut half buried in the dirt of one of my houseplants. That made twelve.

When you're working with numbers, and you have a two-digit number, you add the two digits to decide what the number/ message is. Well, the number was twelve, so one plus two equals three, and three is the number of joy. Ha ha! Certainly true. What joy was all of this! The joy of possibilities. Joy in the consideration that we're not limited, and just the delicious joy of play, of fun, of smiling and connecting to the Universe and its deep grace and presence. And perhaps with all this playfulness, Disney was involved.

Exercise
Make a Happiness List

This exercise comes from my book, *What Color Is Your Slipcover?* I created the exercise to encourage the use of environment to support happiness. It is totally appropriate as an exercise here for I'm talking about raising vibrations, being in touch with your passion, becoming aware of what you love and how carefully you've placed what you love in your life.

Making this list is quite simple. And I bet it's something you haven't done in a long time. Do it when you have relaxed time. Sit with your writing tool, and journal, and list things that really bring you great happiness. Let your list be as long as it wants to be. It will feel so good to even get in touch with the things that you choose.

The advantages of doing this list are endless. What I like about it is how much it can get you back in touch with yourself. It also, can be a wonderful reference for you when you're saying yes, and not enjoying yourself. It means you are saying yes to things that don't even come close to being on your list! Good old self-betrayal, or not being able to say no, or taking care of everybody else. As you do the list, be very honest with yourself. This exercise is not meant to entertain. It's meant to connect with the self.

Notice, when you are finished, how many things on your list do not cost you money!

Here's my list of things that make me happy as a reference:

Time with friends	Feeling clear
Animals of all kinds	Knowing
Travel	Coming home
New learning	Driving
Connection	Discovery
Intimacy	New ideas
Creativity	Wellness
Vacation in Canada	Dancing
Family	Designing
Feeling strong	Beautiful colors
Community	Listening to music
Kayaking	Hiking
Dong my yoga	Mentoring
Making love	Trees and rocks and water
Reading	Going out to dinner
Going to the movies	Buying a great outfit

Sound like the person sharing these stories? You betcha! I am very happy

Love, Denny

CHAPTER TEN

Lightbulbs and Ahas!

So many possibilities exist
between the question and the actual moment of action. It's the
listening in our silence
That brings us to the ways to proceed.
A feeling in our gut, And a knowing that "All is Well."

This chapter wanders because it is important. It tries to convince you to listen, to be silent, so you can hear what's coming through. It needs patience, it needs determination and strangely enough it demands letting go.

My friend, Bill and I planted two red maple trees in the yard of our church as a celebration of our friendship. The church was Interfaith and had an impressive focus toward community and freedom that we both found very precious. We had met there, so we figured it was a perfect place for us to outwardly express our friendship. We planted the trees on a beautiful, sunny spring day with the help of his girlfriend, Linda. We chose fairly mature trees, so we had quite a struggle getting the large root balls into the holes we'd dug. When we got them standing straight and tall, we sighed in relief! In no time Linda and Bill were on their way. They had other things to do.

I couldn't bring myself to leave. I wanted to wallow in the new landscape with our gifts adding a new texture. I also, seemed to feel like there was something left to do. But what I didn't know.

I decided to hang out and see what the feeling was about, to see if anything would occur to me. I laid on my back on the cool grass and just stared up at all the blue sky. I gazed for awhile, and from time to time raised my head to take in the sweet red maples we'd planted. No insight came, only my delight. I wondered what I was searching to do; what was keeping me there other than the joy of the moment. There was something.

I decided to meditate and see if I would get some message. An entire hour went by. I think I even dozed a bit, and finally the light bulb flashed. Do a ritual! "Hmmm, I thought. Why don't I circle each tree separately? I'll walk counter-clockwise around each tree three times." That made me smile. What was I inventing? I circled the way I designed it, blessing each trunk as I walked. And when I was finished, I definitely felt complete.

Saying "Good bye" for the moment, I got in my car to leave, but it all was too much fun. I had to tell someone this story. I knew my friend, Liz would resonate with the experience, so I turned toward Doylestown to see if I could find her. She a stationery store in town, and I could often sneak in and share some fun.

Liz listened to my story of the planting, and grinned broadly. When I finished my tale, she said, "You have to go back!"

"Why?" I asked.

"You're not done." She said. "You have to walk around each tree three times counter clockwise!"

I was stunned. "I already did." I said. "But, why did I do that?" She had repeated exactly what I'd done.

"It's an old Indian custom," she said. "It assures that the trees will live and grow."

I roared that I could get so right-on about what to do! It had been hard to trust the energy that indicated there was more to do, but Liz was certainly affirming my ritual almost to the letter!

I loved the connection I was feeling. I knew I had to find Liz. She was the one that would know. I was feeling so smart, and really filled with awe and this process I was in. Yep, Liz had to playback my ideas with her wonderful conviction. Someday I won't need that so much!

So, the "Aha" moment in this case was when I suddenly had a strong, clear thought, of what I might do to celebrate those pretty trees that were now in the ground. "Aha's" can change your course of action, make things clearer, easier, or even explain how to make something sacred. You might be surprised that a particular idea has so much power, but the power is the magnet to tell you "keep going." If you're open and assume what's coming is relevant (a little cliff jumping here), you'll know just what to do. The trick for me is to hear the "aha" and trust that it is a message, a possibility.

Messages can come in all realms of your life, when you're dealing with a relationship, creativity, or resolving some issue within yourself. Sometimes the message asks you to risk or experiment in some unfamiliar way. That is scary, but if you're open, and it works, it will make life delicious and juicy.

Often, I'm too busy or living in an unconscious way to even see the light bulb go off or hear the "Aha." I know I'm unconscious when I'm not getting any hits of intuition! It's time to unwind my body and mind and start saying, "YES!" to possibilities. "Clear the decks and get still!"

I have had some very profound "Aha!" moments. Sometimes they've come when I've simply been struggling with a problem, a place to begin, even a forgotten name. The light bulb flashes, and I remember or get a new idea, a new possibility. I feel it in my body.

I love to watch children when they have an "aha" moment. The just light up. Whoever used the light bulb, as a cartoonist's symbol of those moments was a genius. The author, Sam Keen would say that it's like trusting the world is walking beside you and whispering in your ear. But the time has to be spent sometimes in stillness to "hear." The story of my first surgery frames this concept well. It held a lot of those vibes.

To begin I'll tell you that for the most part I've always been quite healthy. My body has rarely gotten in the way of my work. But a time came that it did. It was at a meeting of a local women's club, when I was preparing to give a talk on design. I suddenly had an unbearable pain in my groin and knew to take my leave and cancel my talk. I also knew I couldn't drive so I called my son, David and went to the emergency room of the nearest hospital.

After some initial x-rays and some probing, I was advised that there was a cyst in spasm on my right ovary, and immediate surgery was advised. My head was spinning. Surgery was not on my radar screen. I prepared to say, "no," and reject such radical, invasive therapy. But instead I relaxed a bit and telephoned some friends and professionals whose opinions might be helpful. When I finally calmed down to sort it all out, the consensus was to go ahead and get the cyst removed. I thanked my cohorts and surrendered, asking them for prayers and energy.

Considering my feelings about surgery, these deliberations were not easy. One of the downsides of what was happening was so little time for me to prepare myself emotionally. Struggling with my fear, a light bulb went off, and I found myself remembering a magazine article that I'd filed a long time ago. The article was written by a horticulturist, whom had separated a very pot-bound split-leafed philodendron plant and the event had been quite eye opening. He had feared the plant might not survive the surgery so he hung around it the night before muttering what he was going to do and even probing with his hand where he might do the cut. He recognized that he was talking to the plant which made him smile. Lo, and behold when he approached the plant the next morning, it had laid itself open along the line he had indicated. He was stunned at the connection he had made.

I had loved this story when I read it some 20 years ago, and filed it away. It seemed amusing that I was remembering it in a hospital room far away from my file drawer. There was a strong possibility, I thought, that this memory had resurfaced as intuition. Was I receiving the suggestion that I could communicate with my body the same way? I decided to trust that random information as one of my approaches to this operation.

I decided to talk to my body in the same way that gentleman had talked to his plant. I described how we (my body and I) could work together. I really got into it suggesting that we trust and support the surgery, give up the cyst without resistance, and heal quickly and easily. Then, I passed my hand over the place of incision. I couldn't believe I was doing it, but it's what he did. And I certainly had felt an "Aha," when I remembered the article.

I've always dreaded surgery, so I needed to be creative to get me through. I consulted with the surgeon and asked if I could bring my amethyst crystal and some music into the operating room (These ideas had come through other magazine articles!). He was open, and my walkman and crystal were fetched. I decided to have powerful music, so David brought me my *Amadeus* tape. When everything was in place I felt complete, and fell fast asleep. Can you imagine? The support I'd created made me feel so safe, that I had a good night's sleep!

When I awakened, procedures began, and I was wheeled into the operating room. Orderlies helped me place my crystal and start my music, and I was sent off to sleep. When I woke up at the end of the surgery, it was very strange that the entire staff in the room, including my surgeon, was chuckling. I was very fuzzy, so I could not make sense of any of it. But once I gained some grounding I asked what was so funny.

The surgeon told me first that the surgery had been a success and the cyst was benign. Then he chuckled and said that I had been smiling through the entire operation!

"You're joking," I said.

"No, we're not. We were truly amused." The surgeon said.

Others in the room nodded in agreement.I was baffled.

When my son, Carl, called from California I was still mulling over an explanation of what had transpired. I shared it with him.

"Oh Mom, I totally understand, he said. "You weren't there!"

After a good laugh on that one, I assured him that I had an incision to prove precisely where I'd been.

"Well," he said, "I was very upset that I could't be there, so I left my office while you were in surgery and went out to my motorbike. I put you on the back of the bike, and we took a ride up through the mountains and down by the ocean. You threw back your head and laughed all the way. You were not present at the surgery."

I had never heard of such a thing! It was an explanation of possibility that had never occurred to me before. I'd left my present reality, gotten away from the stress, and enjoyed myself.

I now know that this is called shape-shifting. I thought about how it happened. Perhaps I had moved to a higher vibration level through all my preparation and trust, and that had brought me to new possibilities; ones that meant I could leave my body on the operating table. And Carl had taken me away to play with him. I knew I believed it was possible, and the staff had certainly confirmed my state of being. Finding out that I had done it with Carl's help was a gift that would again change my way of being forever.

Well, all I did worked to my benefit. I healed from the surgery very quickly and felt overwhelmed with gratitude for all of my epiphanies and growth and for having a son with such creativity and belief. As I look back, the surgery really turned out to be a minor incident. My new experiments and experiences were much more important, and brought me to many behavior changes, especially talking to my body all the time! And by the way, this is what I mean when I say everything can be a gift.

My choice to not go into fear, but instead to trust myself, the surgeons, and my intuitions had been golden. Speaking with my friends had helped my feelings of vulnerability and isolation, not to mention helping me make a sound choice. The crystal and music were perfect. I was delighted with all I'd done, and felt very empowered and recognized such an experience of growth rather than something to get through. Instead of taking the role of victim, which is easy to do, I opted differently.

I shared this story later with a mother of two, who was approaching the birth of her third child. Her first two births had been very painful, and she dreaded this one. After listening, the light bulb went off for her. She saw the possibility of making this birth experience different that the last two. She actually wrote a script of how she wanted her upcoming birth to be and rehearsed it over and over until she knew it would became her reality.

At the end of her simple delivery she said she was lifted by an energy that made her feel like dancing. The ripple effect of my story continued because when her eighty-five year old mother-in-law heard the story, she was so impressed that she decided to try it in her own life by manifesting an easy death experience. She now believes that she will manifest a painless, beautiful passing that will be filled with energy.

Following the impulse is powerful. Taking charge of what life offers us, and trusting that we can create the outcome we want is totally life changing. To continue bombarding you with this concept I will tell you how another such incident happened one afternoon when I was sitting out in the sun meditating on a sore throat that I was experiencing. My mind played with the idea that there could be other ways to heal. I suddenly imagined a triangle sitting in the spot of pain in my throat. The triangle was purple.

"Wouldn't it be great," I thought, "If we could imagine different colorful shapes in different parts of our body when we needed healing. They would act as medicine. What a great thing that would be!"

That evening I was having dinner with friends and I shared my thought. "Wouldn't it be amazing?" I said, "if the concept that we have everything within us to heal included such things as imagining triangles, pyramids, circles in concert with color to change molecules or shift energy?"

Marie laughed. "You're so psychic." She said. She shared news of how that very day, she had heard of a seminar where a chiropractor was lecturing on just such a process. The seminar was being given up Dr. Paul Mychaluk, who had created an alternative therapy around information channeled to him over the years on diverse shapes that he calls matrix. They are visualized on the appropriate place in the body while you mentally run the shape through a specific spectrum of colors. He also suggests sound as an accompanying tool whether it's you singing, or you listening to music. I've now used his therapy over and over again quite successfully. It especially helps me with fatigue. I tell you about it for it's one more example of an impulse I followed that brought about an expansion of understanding as well as an affirmation that when something occurs to me in thought, I need to listen.

If you're not convinced as yet to follow your own impulses, let me continue! All through writing my first book I received guidance. When I finished the book *What Color Is Your Slipcover?* I conferred with my agent about the process we would use to find a publisher.

She described how we would work on the proposal to get it strong, and then she would send it out to ten publishers hoping to find an interested buyer. She would not share what publishers she was choosing for our first round.

The process began, and I went on with my life. A few weeks later I was going into a Barnes and Noble and passed a table of "Books on sale." Stopping to scope it out, I was drawn to a very beautiful garden book. It had an exquisite layout using lots of colorful illustrations. I couldn't put it down it was so beautiful.

Now, I don't garden, but I still was considering buying this book! Why? It made no sense, but the impulse was too great. I bought it promising myself it would at least go on my nightstand, so I could continue to appreciate the book.

About two days later my agent called saying that Rodale and an editor there, Ellen Phillips, were looking at the book. She coached me to not get excited because, "they take forever to decide," but advised that the process had begun!

When I got off the phone the light bulb flashed again. I ran up to the bedroom. Yep, Rodale had published the garden book, and Ellen Phillips was the editor! This was getting easy. I knew Rodale would purchase the book. It was obvious.

Time did drag a bit, but one day a cardinal sat forever outside my window. I just enjoyed him until suddenly, the light bulb flashed again. I went to my "Animal Speak" book and looked up cardinal. It had so much to say around the number 12. That day it was April

4th. I counted from the 4th and knew I would hear of their desire to purchase my book on April 16^{th,} and I did!

Listening, considering, knowing, following the impulse, the sudden information of what to do, or how to proceed is the way it's done. The "aha" moment is a blessed surging that comes from within like a wave and offers new answers. It happened when I decided to ask to see the owl, or found myself speaking to a tulip, or yes, circling a tree three times counter clockwise. I call it being in the flow and it's truly blessed. You can play this game just the way I'm writing it down, or find your own way. It's yours as easily as it's mine to listen, act and co-create. And yes, for life to be juicy!

Exercise
Getting More Intuitive

How do we do it? How do we make that voice, that idea, come through so loud and clear that we trust it and feel safe to act on it?

By practicing. By being centered enough to realize that a new possibility, an idea, an instruction has occurred that is relative to what you're deliberating, and then acting on it. Trusting that it's intuition, input, guidance, and seriously integrating it into your choices.

Start by wondering about the route you're taking when you're driving.

Are you intuiting an accident ahead, a traffic jam? Either turn on the radio to check it out, or try an alternative route and see if it matters.

Ask for guidance, and then be relaxed enough to hear it. It may come with a voice, an announcement, a conversation, an article in a magazine you suddenly were drawn to open or buy. Practice asking. Practice trusting what you get. Start small and get the feelings connected to intuition. Take in the successes and congratulate yourself. Ask. Listen. Trust. Act. Doing this over and over will begin to grow your intuition. Notice when you do intuit who is calling. Do a lot of assuming that intuition is the cause.

Journal your successes, or just create a list, so you don't forget to practice, and you don't forget that you've been successful, that it does work. And good luck!

CHAPTER ELEVEN

Forgiveness and Transcendence

I managed forgiveness
And it brought me freedom
And I had thought that what I did in the first place
Was freedom!
And then I prayed for more understanding and got it!
And found freedom.
Perhaps it's all free-will!
And that's the treasure

I don't know about you, but I really love New York City. I've contemplated living there. Certainly visiting New York, is the best. When my friend Linda, offered to include me in her invitation to attend New York's, Halloween Costume Ball at the Metropolitan Museum of Art, there was little to debate. We decided we would skip costumes and instead dress to the nines. We even opted to take a limo. True extravagance.

The big night arrived and everything fell into place. As we pulled up to the main entrance, we were dazzled by the costumes parading in front of us. There were animals, flowers, buildings, mystical characters, anything and everything! We pushed through the crowds, gave our tickets and found ourselves just plain gawking at all the amazing innovations. The entire place was so alive! Wild music was blasting down the halls from the Egyptian Room

And it was hot! It was October, but New York was in the midst of a powerful heat wave. Air conditioners offered no relief. In spite of the heat we were determined to enjoy ourselves. We were grinning like Cheshire cats. Deciding to dance we entered the crowded dance floor. Suddenly the music shifted to a different rhythm and a melody that was dissonant, strange and unappealing. We tried, but couldn't catch the beat and make it work.

We gave up and made our way off the dance floor. Walking toward us was a handsome gentleman in a black tuxedo balancing two glasses of champagne. He seemed amused at our chagrin.

"What's your problem?" he asked smiling.

"It's the choice of music." I said. "We can't dance to this. It has no rhythm." My comment seemed to amuse him as he handed Linda the two glasses of champagne. Turning and opening his arms to me without a word, he took me in his arms and we began to dance. We dipped, and swirled in total concert with the music! He wasn't having any difficulty. He took us in and out with ease and grace. His lead was strong, and I followed easily.. On and on we danced. It seemed like a dream as he led me around the dance floor.

Well, remember it was a very hot evening, and we'd been dancing awhile. I really began to mind the heat. My entire body was covered with sweat, my heart was racing, and my breathing was desperate. But I couldn't bring my-self to end the dance. It was too wonderful. I'd never felt so elegant, so seized in dance. So I prayed! Really! Prayed on the dance floor! It sounds hysterical, doesn't it? But I found I didn't want to stop!

"Just let me finish this dance!" I prayed.

I didn't care what came after. Anything would be okay, If I could just finish the dance. Almost immediately as we continued, my pulse came back to normal, my breathing slowed and my body cooled down completely! As I danced on I was well aware of the transcendence that had happened, and it made me feel quite giddy.

Finally the dance ended. My partner thanked me, handed me his business card and hurried off. He was soaked to the skin. Before he left, I thanked him profusely. When I got back to Linda, she greeted me with eyes wide open in awe. "How did you do that?!" she said.

"I'll tell you later," I said huffing and puffing, "but right now I will say that this was one of the most amazing moments of my life."

I never saw Sergio (his name was on his card) again, but having his card was perfect. I knew I had to let him know the gift of his dance. The next week I shopped card department upon card department until I found a perfect card. On it I wrote how much the dance had meant to me. To emphasize it I copied the wonderful words of a favorite Hafiz poem from his book. You probably know it. The title is I Saw you Dancing,

I Saw You Dancing

I saw you dancing last night on the roof
Of your house all alone.

I felt your heart.

I saw you whirling
Beneath the soft bright rose
That hung from an invisible stem in
The sky,

So I began to change into my best clothes
In hopes of joining you

Even though I live a thousand miles away.

And if
You had spun like an immaculate sphere
Just two more times,

Then bowed again so sweetly to
The east,

You would have found me
Standing so near
And letting you lift me into your Arms.

I saw you dancing last night near the roof
Of this world.

I feel your soul in mine
Calling.

HAFIZ

I signed it 'Denny" and mailed it, putting no return address on the envelope. I was complete. I knew what the dance was about. I had learned surrender and transcendence, states that I had never really understood before. To this day I smile broadly whenever I think of it.

I adored how I had moved in his arms, how I'd felt complete union with his lead, And then I loved how I'd slid into that moment of letting go like a cat sliding through narrow fence rails, and how delicious it was, even more delicious on the other side of that fence!

That experience and its learning has served me well. To illustrate let me segue to another story that began on a day when I was as out of sorts as I could get. It was a Sunday and I was attending an event with friends. I was definitely glad I was going, It was a beautiful day, sunny, fresh, alive. but somehow once I got to the event everyone was annoying me. I felt very angry inside and stressed without knowing why. I took a seat near the front of the room. A woman who usually rattles me, sat down with a cheery "hello!." I could hardly answer her I was so out of sorts.

That mood (I don't even want to call it mine) continued throughout the program, as I kept struggling to even sit there with presence. Finally everyone was up and moving about, and I was relieved.

I greeted some friends, didn't stay in any conversation long and hoped I would get through this ridiculous situation. In the midst of this strange vacuum I overheard my name and turned to witness a friend singing my praises. I blushed as if they knew my mood. That even piqued me. It took every ounce of control for me to be civil to anyone.

What in the world was going on? I had never felt so insensitive. Who was I? It got quite clear that I must get out of there and regroup. I had managed civility so far. If I'd understood the source of my pain, perhaps I could have shifted, but I was clueless why I was in such a funk.

Driving home, I tried to sort out the whole experience. These feelings and behavior were new to me. It resembled past memories of how my father looked and acted when he'd had too much to drink. I wondered if he'd always felt the way I was feeling . . . like all of the time. Perhaps it was why he drank! I had never known the source of his alcoholism. For years he tried to resolve his drinking without success, and it made me pity him, and at other times hate him. Continuing my deliberation as I drove, I began to wonder if my mood was in truth the way my father always felt. What it would be like to walk around in his skin feeling that way everyday? No wonder he desired the numbness of alcohol. I escaped by leaving the scene. He would have had to always be leaving, separating. What a hell that would be!

All this awareness was huge. I was seeing years of a tortured father in new ways. Realizing that this man, whom I did love deeply, had felt that kind of pain most of his life, felt devastating.

I began to cry. I cried rivers in that car driving home. This state of being that I was in could be an amazing possibility that would explain Dad's lifetime of struggle. As I cried, a powerful feeling of understanding and forgiveness came over me. I began feeling relief, the end of a journey, a change of perception, tenderness and transformation.

I went to bed that night feeling changed and so much lighter. In the middle of the night the phone rang. There was no one there. "Hello . . . hello," I said feeling relief and annoyance.

Miffed I replaced the receiver and went back to sleep. When I wakened in the morning I remembered the call. And pushed *69 to hear the number that had called. It was unfamiliar, but I wrote it down.

It was a warmish spring morning with the sun shining. I had a long list of things to do. I ate my bowl of oatmeal standing at the kitchen window (something I hardly ever do). Outside on the lawn baby robins were receiving intense flying instructions from a doting mother. It made me smile, and reminded me how mother had watched baby robins leaving their nest the night my father passed over. She said she used it like a departing meditation.

Standing at the window, I smiled at how amazing that synchronicity had been. But wait! My mind picked up a fast pace of awareness as I grabbed my calendar. My God, today actually was the exact date of my father's passing, June 6th!

Stunned, I grabbed for the phone and dialed the number that had interrupted my sleep. A few rings and my friend Barbara's voice answered telling me that she was not available but to leave a message. The phone calling was Barbara's cell phone! I never used it when I called her. Quickly I dialed her land phone to ask her whether she knew where her cell phone was, and had she used it to call me in the middle of the night?

"No," she replied, and went to find it. Returning she announced that her cell phone was *turned-off* and sitting on her kitchen counter quite safe and sound.

Now Barbara knows of my experiences. You remember she's the one that joined me to ask the bees to leave. Her response was very clear. "When did you get the call?" I remembered for I'd looked at my digital clock just after the whole interruption happened. "It was 2:37AM," I said.

I nearly dropped the phone as I said it for it was to the moment, the exact time he died. We sat silent for some very long moments. "I'd be vigilant today, Sweetie." She said. "I think your dad is trying to reach you."

I felt such gratitude that she was available and able to hear and respond to these circumstances. I agreed. I knew I was in the midst of another one of *those* days. I wondered if yesterday's experience of forgiveness had brought my father closer, or was the universe packaging this as a healing process?

I looked at the clock and realized it was time to move on with my day. I had an appointment with a design client set for 12:30 PM. I continued as normally as I could (trusting and surrendering completely) and proceeded to my car. Driving up the highway I pondered the morning's script. It felt strangely sweet and mysterious. Cutting through my reverie was the thought that I might be running late. Passing a large digital clock, I saw that my timing was a bit close. It was 12:22 PM, and I had another ten miles to go.

12:22!! Yikes! That was my father's birthdate! Now I knew something was going on. I was awake, smiling and staying tuned. Surely a new mystery was unfolding.

I arrived at my client's home in the midst of heavy rain. We were going to address her kitchen renovation in an old style farmhouse. We greeted each other and got ready to move past the heavy plastic dividing the heavy work and dust from the rest of the house. I had lots of sample books to carry, and as I bent over to grasp the pile a huge pain surged in my chest. I froze not saying a word. Immediately my father's voice came through with great clarity and intensity. Of course it was only for my ears but I listened carefully.

"Do not be concerned." he said. "You're absolutely fine. You are experiencing a heart opening (was it generated by my forgiveness and compassion yesterday?) You will have more pain. Just move calmly and patiently through it without worry. Be as positive as you can."

About 11 years before, I had experienced what was called a slight heart attack. I didn't feel well one morning and ended up driving myself to the doctor's office. I was hospitalized, and put through many tests and treatments to come up with a diagnosis of a mild heart attack. It was an intense time with a concerned family, although my son, Carl, told me he knew it was nothing! After some weeks of recuperation and thought time, I wondered if I'd had a heart opening instead. I'd read a detailed description in Barbara Brennan's book, *Hands of Light*, claiming that a heart opening was painful and often misdiagnosed, that literally it's the heart opening more through a person rising to the challenges of growth and change. It had been just after my divorce, so it really made sense.

I am sharing that passage of my life to make you aware that I had been through the experience of thinking I'd had a heart attack and then led to discover that instead I'd had a heart opening. During the time of dealing with that I was intimately shown that I was fine by a sign.. You see it was Christmas Day, and I was in the kitchen alone preparing the turkey for roasting, I reached inside of this gorgeous Christmas offering to remove the gizzards, heart and neck.

When I withdrew the packet there were two hearts inside instead of one. I stood amazed, grounded in the moment, grateful and stunned. I accepted and believed its message.

I knew it could have been just a fluke that there were two hearts in that packer, but on this journey you know when it is a sign and when it isn't! I knew I was being shown that I was fine, that my heart was perfectly healthy, just more open. I cried. It was another moment when I knew I was not alone, that I was being cherished for being on the journey. It was rich to stand there so held in a reality that I trusted., Then as my life moved on, I continued my medication and doctor's visits for a while, and finally discontinued everything. Feeling so held. I became stronger in every moment of acceptance.

So, returning to this story, it seemed to be adding up to the fact that today I was receiving a very intimate message through many different synchronistic moments, that I was having a heart opening, not a heart attack. I vowed to trust the message that was coming even though there was nothing else supporting the possibility than his communication.

I completed the design appointment confidently, helped myself by deep breathing, and a vow not to panic. After driving myself home I went to bed and stayed there or around the house for the next four days. Just staying loose and taking care of me allowed time to contemplate what had transpired. Barbara called often validating what was happening and checking into my energy.

What was it all about? What had opened my heart? Why was my father guiding this event? Charting the moments from my unfamiliar mood and on to awareness and challenge, I could see some very powerful learning and healing. Was this completion with my father as I forgave him for the impact on me of his addiction? I guess only time would tell, but for now the layer I had removed was huge. And I had transcended anger, grief, and fear.

I remained in bed a few days, going in and out of some fatigue and discomfort. Then my life moved on in new ways, accompanied by a now grateful heart. I was proud of my trust and grateful to all my escorts, the owl, the squirrels, the tulip, the snake, the impulses, and how they all continued to wake me up to my power . . . to a bigger reality., and the knowing that "All is well!"

Exercise
Creating Affirmations

Changing your beliefs is not easy. They came into your life at big moments, from authorities and people you really trusted or loved, and they've been alive for a long time. Unfortunately that doesn't make them right, wrong, nor permanent. And you can choose to change any or all. Affirmations are a wonderful way to help change as long as you are open to their change. But part of the affirmations working is you *believing* they will and *feeling* it can be so.

Your brain will trust a *new belief* if you affirm it often enough. Wanting to ingrain a new concept into your subconscious mind can happen by repeating an affirmation often (!) for it is you continually informing your brain and all your cells that your new belief is so.

Typical affirmations are:
I am worthy.
I love myself.
I am perfectly capable.
I am lovable.

I am safe.

They can also be much more specific. You can create any affimation you want. Once you've decided what your affirmations are going to be, you repeat them every day over and over again. Morning is a perfect time for the exercise., when you're relaxed, open, energetic, and clear. Say each one with great emphasis. Choose your language so you're not, vague, insecure, hesitant. The more positive, clear, confident, and sure you can be, the better. Your cells and your brain will believe what youare saying if you say it as if you believe it. They won't know any differently. Trust me!

Do not use negatives in affirmations. "I am not afraid!" is using a negative. Instead use "I am totally safe!" or "I am without fear!" Your language is very important. Also, use the advice I gave about praying. Affirm in the positive as though it already is true.

Re-evaluate your affirmations often, adding new ones, making sure there's no conflicting statements. Eliminate or change affirmations carefully for you want to be clear with this process, not chaotic. AND REMEMBER TO TRUST (BELIEVE) that affirmations work.

In closing I suggest you "act as if" your affirmation or request is answered, your body is healed, your perfect relationship is here, your abundance is present WITH GREAT GRATITUDE!

CHAPTER TWELVE

A Butter Churn?
A Sycamore Tree?

Oh! It is a glorious journey, the upward way,
The amazing discoveries,
The tender moments,
The never expected understanding.
It's falling in love over and over again.

So are you getting there? Are you getting in touch with the beliefs that need to shift, or better put, that you want to shift? Do you feel challenged in letting go? And do you have ways you get your answers? I keep repeating that beliefs are our foundation. What we believe will be what forms and effects everything in our lives including who we are. Do you believe you are worthy, do you believe you're alone, do you believe you're lovable, Do you know it might be time for you to change? Have you decided what is possible? Are you important enough for an owl to come to you when you ask?

Perhaps your answers will change, maybe with these stories. Looking at your journey and your thoughts is a place you must go . . . challenging the stuff you've accepted as your Truth, or making sure you've even considered what's holy for you up to now is important! It's forming you day by day. And it's just so precious to move into a place of wondering and self-examination.

Beliefs and perspectives come from all you've ever been told, lived, loved, experienced, known and held. They are progressive. They hold the essence of every book, every conversation, every connection, every day you've ever lived. They are your heart. Often you don't know exactly what it is you believe. You haven't even thought about it. But I can vouch that you have a list of beliefs that have accumulated regularly and deeply within you.

My first story in this chapter is about what each of us believes is holy (Divine), which is what constitutes a belief. I got a powerful affirmation about my way of approaching ideas and beliefs during a trip with friends, Fran and Carol, to the Barnes Foundation in Philadelphia.

First let me tell you that the Barnes Foundation is an amazing museum that houses the paintings belonging to Barnes, the discoverer of Penicillin. With the fortune that he accrued he collected art of many great masters, Cézanne, Monet, Degas, Renoir, and so on. Barnes loved his art and wanted to share it with the public, so he created a building of many, many rooms and hung most of the art himself. He did so in categories. For instance one room had amazing paintings by great artists where elbows were very prominent. In another room there are sketches and paintings that are primarily portraits of the upper body. This unusual display helps one see the paintings in a new way, and perhaps with some humor!

Fran, Carol and I did not take a guided tour for Carol had led tours at the Foundation often in years past and was able to make our day very rich and fun with what she knew. I had never been to the Barnes Foundation so I was witnessing the collection for the first time. One of my favorite rooms turned out to be the "Christian Room," even though I don't know if I consider myself Christian any more. It was filled with many different styles and perspectives of the Crucifixion and devotion. There were lots of paintings that were traditional icons, paintings done with gold paint, two dimensional style and familiar characters from the Bible.

Carol pointed to an oil painting of a butter churn that was also, in the room. and asked us why we thought that painting had been hung in this particular room? I was as surprised as she was that it was there and took some time to contemplate her question. I wondered whether it was a mistake, or that perhaps some curator had hung it there to fill an empty space. Certainly Carol's question was whether it belonged in the Christian room, or what did we think Barnes was trying to say? It certainly was unorthodox, an object that surprised us.

I know that objects can have a very deep meaning from my work with design clients and students. As you know, I've been an interior designer for years. When I'm designing, I often ask the question "What is Your Most Beloved Object?" I find it helps a person discover what object that they own has the most meaning (is holy) for them, and as a teacher or designer it helps me source some very important information about them that I can reflect back in their home design. Their answers always help me see their priorities and perspectives and then I can use this information to direct their project visually, emotionally, and spiritually.

When Carol asked me the question of the butter churn, I was reminded of "beloved objects," and one in particular. Suzanne, a student of mine said that her beloved object would be a small wooden spoon that had belonged to her Grandmother. Her spoon was quite dried up and even cracked in one place. It was far from elegant and hardly visually beautiful. This gave me great information that Carolyn was very sentimental (because the object had belonged to her grandmother), very practical and loved things that were functional. In her home I saw this reflected in many ways. For example Carolyn had taken a beautiful antique bureau and turned it into a functioning washstand long before it was a trend. And also, Carolyn's object was a spoon, a cooking utensil. She was an awesome cook and grew most of her vegetables. You see her object did represent her so well and suggested to me that she loved practicality, efficiency and creativity. I would be inspired in our work, therefore, to make sure her choices in design, were practical, efficient and creative (perhaps unusually so.) The spoon was not in perfect condition, so I also knew that she did not need things to be in perfect condition. My point in telling you all this is the fact that a wooden spoon was beloved and "sacred" to Carolyn. It was not a crucifix, rosary beads, an old Bible, or anything close to a religious symbol. She found holiness in this well-used spoon.

That made me think that Barnes, also perceived that a butter churn could be as holy as a cross to some people. Fran and Carol loved the story and the reasonable explanation.

We forgot the discussion, went through other rooms of the museum and on to a restaurant nearby for some good food. When we were finished, we found ourselves reviewing our day in the parking lot. Fran was standing beside my car, Carol was sitting in hers. I was inside my car with the sun-roof open.

Fran suddenly asked me, "What is this thing lodged in your sunroof track?" She held up a wooden spoon! I blinked, not understanding how she'd gotten my wooden spoon from my kitchen drawer in her hand in that moment.

"I recognize my spoon." I said, "Where was it?" She pointed to the spot. The only explanation I could come up with was that upon my return from some potluck dinner, I had placed my salad bowl on top of the car to unlock my door. The spoon fell into the track. That wasn't such a big deal, except that we were finding it at a very relevant moment! That was the big deal! I had chosen a wooden spoon as an example! We all had chills. In fact we were quite speechless.

I tell you this story because it embodies so much of the essence of what keeps happening over and over. A thought, question, or concept is reflected almost immediately in the space around. Confirmation comes forward and creates wonder and new belief. This is so much more meaningful for me than doctrine or dogma. I find it powerful when the way I'm holding belief gives way to the experiment and the revelation. It says to me that spirit is in everything, and that every object, being, perspective, moment, activity, and decision may have a message for me about Truth. And it is holy because it is so alive!

The butter churn and the spoon are real things in life that can embody as powerful a message as the crucifixion. The "story of the crucifixion" is holy and it embodies love and service. But that message coming forward in other objects gives everyone the opportunity to touch the same beliefs in another way, one that is not necessarily consecrated by the Church or the Bible, but instead is grounded in life, in that which is functional, that which is mundane but meaningful. It's sets up all of life as being imbued with Divine messages, gifts, helpfulness, lessons and ideas.

In the past I categorized everything just like the paintings at the Barnes. I had my work, my play, my relationships and then my spiritual life. Everything was separate and categorized. I allowed myself and everyone else to be separated by race, economic level, skill, preference, gender, species, everything. There was no integration. No common ground.

But now, I see it differently, that all life is holy and that my beliefs can be embodied in many parts of life. If everything is holy and divine, it includes a smile on a baby's face, the cross someone wears daily, the oak tree standing in my backyard, and a butter churn that someone uses to make butter for their beloved family. Love and service!

And all my beliefs evolve, and join other beliefs about possibilities. They are not my beliefs of five years ago, and they may not be what I'll believe in the future. They'll change again and again as I'm guided, and I respond to the messages of that guidance. I can begin to have a whole new understanding of, healing possibilities, abundance, change, communication, and the unlimited aspect of life itself if I keep opening my beliefs.

At the end of this chapter, I will invite you to decide where you are in terms of your own beliefs. I'll ask you to totally understand and embrace the place you are right now, to not judge yourself or let your ego get involved. You're on a journey just like I, and you won't get there with clarity if you don't self-examine and decide what you believe now. In the exercise I'll ask you to go deep, so you are very clear. It might interfere with some old traditions and dogma or you might find yourself much more committed right where you are.

You will have many Epiphanies that will no longer come from laws, or rules, or books. The human condition might strike you differently. Duality may fade away, and the physical and the spiritual may become one.

Your owl, your tulip, your snake may begin to feel like your kin. Or perhaps you will evolve in some other very magical way that will make life so wonder-full for you. Each time it happens it will be a form of rebirth. You'll be doing it all the time.

I have just turned 70. To celebrate I went out to dinner with my friend, Barbara, to a beautiful outdoor restaurant. It was August, warm and sparkly. We had our usual sharing of stories and views coupled with our oohs and ahhhs over the amazing cuisine. The grounds were exquisite with manicured lawns, huge sycamore trees, bird songs, moonlight and a wandering violin player. Our conversation went to my turning 70 and the way things were forming in my mind from all my reality, how I was coming to a new idea of me. I wanted to have some rebirth in certain parts of my life, and I was searching for the ways to bring it about. The conversation, and the evening felt truly blessed.

When our meal ended we went on to my home as Barbara was spending the night, I got her situated in the guest bedroom and we said good night. Sleep came fast for me and was sweet and deep. It was interrupted around four o'clock by me suddenly opening my eyes and observing a vision of Barbara sitting at the bottom left side of my bed talking to me as if we were still at dinner. As she finished repeating some of the conversation of the night before, she smiled at me, raised her left hand and pointed to the right side of my bed as if to say "Look who's here!" I turned to the right and there standing by my bed looking down at me was my mother. She looked younger, more peaceful and seemed to be saying, "Happy Birthday!" with her eyes.

Then she was quickly gone.

I lay there filled with warmth and huge love. Her appearance was a gift of healing proportions. I fell back to sleep until eight AM when I was awakened by Barbara's real voice calling to ask whether I was awake. I responded that I was and to please come up.

When she entered the room, I laughed. "Welcome back!"

"What do you mean?" she asked.

I told her that she'd been there earlier and repeated the scene as it had unfolded.

"What do you make of it?" She said.

"I don't know yet," I answered, "Although just her appearance seemed like happy birthday and that was enough."

I thought of the setting for our meal of the night before and wondered if I might think of any clues about the message of the visit. I looked in my Ted Andrew's book, *Nature Speak,* to see if there was some significance about the three beautiful sycamore trees. I read that the keynote of the sycamore is nourishment, beauty, new life and new gifts. That the sycamore is often called the ghost tree (!), and with its whitish bark stands out visually in the woods . . . especially at night when the moonlight is strong! He continued that Sycamore energies help prevent atrophy of higher abilities that an individual has brought into this lifetime; a reminder to build on old gifts and to express them in new ways. I found this message so warming and certainly appropriate, it was about rebirth. It partnered so beautifully with the dinner conversation about taking the lid off of some of my old ways of being! So the Sycamore Trees were definitely escorts to the evening. Funny that I had chosen that place for our meal (and not so funny!)

With all the considerations, my final analysis was that my mother's message was of rebirth. Time to do some serious reawakening using all I'd learned and all of my power. Time to examine what needs to change within me and within my life, I will listen carefully to the moments that make my heart expand, and I will push through the ways that hold me back, where I abandon myself. And at 70 I will again begin to move forward.

And you at your age, will also rebirth. Your soul will lead you, train you, challenge you, discipline you. You can picture your soul as a being that's just loving you, sharing with you and rejoicing in your progress, your new discipline, your deeper way of listening, trusting and sharing.

That which you find that is Love,
That is you.
All that you find in your life is you

So what do I think is most important for you to believe in? It's not my choice. What is most holy unequivocally is for you to believe in you, in your power. Perhaps everything is holy. Once you know your answers, move forward into your journey remaining open and contemplative. Expect everyday to bring you new possibilities. Open to new ways of thinking and being. Listen, look, and allow things to become different to change. And be aware. Allow yourself to be guided from inside the wonderful heart that is yours. And do it believing in your power.

Exercise
The Art of witnessing another.

Select a person who you admire, one who you know quite well, that you feel brings an abundance of light to the planet. Who makes a difference, who represents a love presence. Take some time and write your understanding of what they believe, who they are, what they contribute and how. Write as much as you can about who you understand them to be. Even address ways they problem solve, values they live by, goals that they have, and how they are in relationships.

I suggest this not be a list of judgement, but instead let it be you contemplating this person's life in order to examine, take in, understand this life that you admire, this person of worth. Enjoy this exercise. It is very positive, and will make you feel good. It also, will teach you a lot about yourself as well as enjoying the uniqueness of another person.

CHAPTER THIRTEEN

Sourcing From Within

So knowing all you know now,
Do you know what you want?
If you do not . . . that is now your work.
Make use of the connection
And the messages,
Waiting to serve you in every moment.

I have a shiny, red Camry, hybrid. I love it! It's quiet, low on gas, comfortable, and I feel virtuous for having it! Getting into this hybrid provides me with a new kind of experience. It is an environment that senses and gives me feedback on multiple levels all the time. The door unlocks with a click as long as I have the key-object in my purse." I don't have to see it or even hold it in my hand. I just have to have it with me.

And there are many more messengers and assistants. A light turns on at perfect times, an icon on the dashboard shows me any doors that are still open, or any imbalance in my tires. A dial shows me the level of fuel, or the temperature of the engine. The temperature outside is recorded magically; even the temperature inside! I'm shown what gear I'm in and whether the car is "ready" to move. I am made totally aware of all my realities. The rear view mirror has a message about what direction I'm driving, and even adjusts its angle when there is harmful glare. I don't have a GPS, but I know that having one is an experience of accompaniment that is beyond, beyond. If you have one you know the voice and map are so virtual it's as if someone is sitting beside you acknowledging street signs, turns, and route numbers

The entire environment of this car is alive, and gives back to the occupants a multitude of information, support, and yes, guidance. Everything is there one could possibly want to know. You just have to be awake enough to take it in and then process what it means to you and to respond.

Our bodies have these same possibilities. We're not delivered the information by dials and numbers, but feelings that will basically give us just as complete a read. We can feel weakness, temperature, danger, pain, pleasure and symptoms. We can see direction, feel dampness, hear wind, detect energy. We don't even come close to using all of those tools as we occupy this sacred physical vessel.

Our bodies and our cars seem to me to be perfect metaphors of the universe, a big huge environment with all the information and guidance we need! As you've certainly picked up, I've been schooled in this for a long time by all my escorts. My job now is to remember that it's there for me, to ask for what I want, and to respond. That is my key. Your's is to discover it in your own life.

Sometimes knowing all this doesn't guarantee that I remember. I still can numb out and forget that this universe, like my hybrid or my body, is a constant companion. And it's interesting that when I do numb out, my clarity, is gone. I don't receive guidance—I'm no longer in the flow of all possibility. Instead I'm stuck. And if I wake up again, listen to the voices, read the signs, the magic falls easily into place.

An old memory that has come back to me at this moment happened before the story of the owl. It was a small moment, but truly profound and may have been my first encounter with sensing a possibility, although it's hard to track. I was hiking with friends. At about the halfway-point I became exhausted, and wondered if I could finish the hike.

We stopped for a rest, and I stood back, debating what to do. The day was gorgeous, hot with a clear blue sky, the trees and bushes just sparkling. Perfect, except for this lapse I was having into fatigue, I didn't know if I should quit or continue. If I backed out tt might take as much energy to return as it would to proceed slowly. Pondering this, my attention was drawn to a large rock sitting by the side of the path. A seat! I decided I'd sit down It was the perfect size.

As I walked toward it I noticed the rock was saturated with sunlight. I don't know why that hit me because everything was saturated with sunlight! But I was prompted somehow that the sun's energy was being stored in the rock. It was one of the moments when this now familiar voice began to speak to me, whispering that the energy just might be medicine for me.

That's how this awareness began to birth. Up to that moment, rocks were rocks, trees were trees, birds were things that flew around and landed on branches, on and on. I had no perception of them as "alive" companions. My mode was that I would guess as things occurred to me and get information in bits and pieces through miscellaneous thoughts and feelings.

And so I wondered if this rock could give me some of its stored energy. It was worth the try. Without any ceremony, I sat down and imagined myself being filled up with new fuel. I visualized it as clearly as I might visualize my Camry at the pumps getting filled with gas. And it worked! I became wonderfully refreshed and ready to move on. I knew I'd finish the hike.

Now fast forward to 36 years later (now), and me after this mega course in new realities It's the fall of 2008 and I'm having a lot of trouble with my gall bladder. Gall bladder attacks were following fatty meals like periods would occur at the end of sentences. Surgery began to loom closer and closer. I looked for signs, remedies, and rocks (not stones!) to get me healed. Sometimes I shifted the energy for a while, and then I'd forget to be careful. A crab Imperial or sour cream dip would be my downfall, and I'd be back to coping with twenty minute periods of breath-taking pain.

One evening a friend prepared a fabulous lasagna dish for us. As she cooked I wondered about the ingredients, the high percentage of fatty cheeses and beef. Should I take the chance and indulge, or pass and just have saladl?

Within my bones there lives a mighty Italian. Passing up lasagna is like passing up life. My addiction to tomato sauces and cheese won, and I ate every bit of that juicy, rich, sumptuous meal. I was in lasagna heaven. I intended no problems, no punishments.

After eating, Rene and I went to the living room to watch a television program. As time went on, I could feel the tell-tale signs of doom creeping forward in my gut. I was in trouble and began to freeze in place. What in the world was I going to do? It was an attack and following too closely on the heels of a similar one two weeks before. I was scared.

My mind went back through so many of the times I've shared with you when I shifted energy in big and important ways. Most of those times I was alone in the privacy of my own home. This fact seemed to stymie me. I struggled for guidance.

Suddenly a voice in my head said, "Call in Barb's energy."

You've met Barb in these pages. She is critical and precious to this journey. We dispelled the bees. Remember! Barbara is an energy worker professionally and has helped me shift through many difficult moments. I liked the idea of calling her in, but wasn't sure.

"I haven't asked her permission." I thought.

"Trust your relationship," I was told. "Just quietly call to her with your thoughts and ask for what you want.

So, as Rene, and I sat watching a very engrossing television show, another part of me imagined myself speaking to Barb and asking for her assistance to shift my dilemma. Slowly I felt the presence of her energy all around me. I relaxed and did deep breathing. My body completely let go of the pain, and I returned to a feeling of safety and trust.

Were you able to visualize all of this happening, Rene and I maintaining a lovely evening as I'm struggling inwardly, and calling in Barb? It's two distinct realities going on at the same time? And it worked! The pain slowly disappeared, as I finished out a great evening of friendship and a deep healing.

Both of these friends know this story. I told Rene a few days later about it, and I told Barb one evening during a conversation about how everything we need is within our reach. The universe is just waiting for us to direct the energy. All that's required is asking!

And sometimes instead the universe is standing by to inform us, as it did when Roger's daughter Alison was born. (Chapter 4) That time was more of a reflection and a message of something coming to be, showing me that all is known. It's not unlike May 14th, 2008 when my son, Carl, called at 3 AM to tell me that I had a new grandson, Daniel Daikeler. I was ecstatic and went back to sleep. At 7:00 AM, a newborn fawn wobbled out of my woods mirroring the wonder of birth. Over and over again, what is going on is mirrored so we can see that all is known, we are in concert together.

One more scenario that illustrates how available and responsive this awaiting energy is was one morning recently when I woke up inspired with all I had to do. My excitement vanished quickly as I began experiencing a great deal of vertigo. I didn't have a cold, I wasn't dizzy, but I felt as though I was going to topple over if I leaned the least bit sideways.

That afternoon I was to be leading a worship celebration, something I was really looking forward to doing. I moved about carefully hoping this predicament would pass. No messages were coming in, and I didn't seem to have any resources other than my intentions.

Floundering I decided to pull an angel card. Two slipped into my hand, and I accepted both. One was "Transformation" and the other was "Creativity."

I took some time to meditate on each, and decided I was being told to trust that this was some new moment for me, one where creativity might get me through. I got dressed and prepared to go. One of my worries was about the drive, so I promised myself I'd travel with my cell phone just in case I needed to ditch my plans.

The vertigo seemed to subside as I drove, perhaps because it was the car moving rather than me. I worried what would happen when I did have to move again. Wanting to bolster my confidence or heal the situation before I was up at the mic, I began to search for some sign. My attention was drawn to the woods along the highway which was dense with so many beautiful trees, all starkly bare in the December cold. How balanced they appeared. How grounded. "No vertigo there," I thought.

The light went on. That was it! The tree people were showing me their balance. Perhaps I could have some of their energy. I reminisce how that moment was like my experience with the rock (or what the native Americans would call the stone people.

As I drove, I began to visualize the picture of a tree inside of me. I pictured it tall, very straight with branches deliberately and strongly protruding from all sides. I saw roots that went way down into the ground providing stability, strength, confidence and power to the tree. Those feelings began to creep in and empower me. I visualized myself strong, straight and balanced. "Thank you." I muttered. "Thank you, thank you," over and over again

It was working! When I arrived at my destination I slipped into a meditation session that was about to begin, knowing it was an opportunity for me to seal this phenomenon. I took a seat, made my posture very straight and balanced, closed my eyes and visualized myself standing now *within* a most amazing trunk of a tree that seemed to just be there for me. It had powerful branches and leaves. I saw light coming down through the branches. At first it seemed like a street lamp that was casting shadows of my fluttering leaves onto the trunk. Then the light became moonlight, which not only lit all the top leaves, but cast a magnificent tall shadow across the earth. I was shape-shifting to learn all the tree had to offer.

The vertigo was gone. Creativity and visualization had transformed a very difficult state. I had resourced everything I needed. The tall, stately trees had reminded me of my possibilities standing so firmly planted by the side of the road. I got all the signals I needed.

Just to review with you, I have remembered to ask for help from all the beings around me. I have learned that the possibility of help is always present. I trust that the answers will come, that I will be shown again who I am and who I can be.

The best way to end this sharing is to complete my opening story. You see I began writing this chapter sitting in the waiting room of the Toyota dealer. I had taken my composition book to begin this, my last chapter. As I waited for my car the white page stared at me quite empty. I found myself writing. ordinary things as though you and I were in conversation. It made me yawn and would have done the same to you. The page remained blank. I remained stumped.

Sitting across from me was a woman, dialoging with a maintenance person about a malfunctioning sensor on her dashboard. She was explaining that when she looked at the car's clock she got the temperature instead of the time. The two of them were going on and on. The only thing interrupting their dialogue was another voice, a man talking about the *sensor* in his car. I turned to the man sitting closest to me and laughingly remarked, that the topic of sensory was certainly up for the day. He laughed and agreed.

The light went on! Turning back to my empty page I began to think of my Camry and its sensory abilities, an environment that could tell me anything I needed to know in order to drive and be comfortable and safe in my car. "Not unlike the universe that I'm writing about," I thought. And there it was. The story I needed in order to begin the ending! It was a perfect metaphor to wrap it up.

How neatly I'd been set up again. The conversations around me were a perfect beginning. The connections continue as I respect that this book has been writing itself. Sensory was the perfect place to go. It wraps up the story so well and shares reminders of our wonder-full life every day on the planet.

And so I conclude with encouragement—encouragement to you to experiment and become present to this experience in your own life. I will also, remind you that in order to take this journey, you must be filled with entitlement. None of this richness can be yours without your feeling that you deserve it. You must be willing to explore and risk, and you must be willing to trust. Trusting your thoughts, your impulses, your questions, enough to listen and act upon them. And in doing that, all will be answered. All of your creativity will emerge and accompany you to great power and joy. Walk deep and be awake. It is the greatest way to guarantee every possibility, every desire, every need being met in every moment.

God, the Universe, Source, the Creator, Allah…blesses us all and connects us to All in every moment.

Appendix

We can put the boat in the water
And we can get in
But without the oars (our tools)
We cannot nearly manage the current...

If you have found that all the experiences that are coming toward you at this time are a bit mind-boggling, or even seem "flaky." The material in this section might be helpful. Perhaps you are getting too much advice as you are talking to others. It is important to share, *and it is also imperative to begin thinking from your own heart, your own perspective.* I found in the beginning of all these synchronicities I wasn't making new choices from my own Truth. It was difficult. Could I really trust myself, "the power within me" instead of the plethora of instructions, or statistics, which were literally bombarding me just like they do you? We read so much about how to be, what to eat, how to exercise, how to sleep, live, relate. Considering that we might know what's best for our own selves is looked at as grossly absurd! I believe this is our greatest work for it is time to gain confidence and begin choosing for ourselves.

I found that I needed to encourage in myself a different way of thinking things through. There were times I did some therapy to see where I was coming from whether it was from my story, or a healthier place of trusting and knowing just what I wanted. Sometimes I would take a workshop or attend a lecture without the approval of others. Sometimes I would read a book by a front-runner or spiritual teacher, or sometimes a not so popular lecturer or author. At first I put all my trust in them. But then, as my intuition began to develop I realized I had to get my mind around what was best for me.

I found that oracles helped for zeroing in on something or giving me a nudge, but my heart and mind, and my feelings were still my most important place to live from. I was the one that had to make my choices of what to believe and what to accept as my Truth. Nothing and no one else should be telling me what to do, or how to be, or even who to be.

Tools help you get to that centered place of knowing who you are and what is best. Oracles are amazing. They literally pick up your energy and hand it back to you in a sign. The same is true of your thoughts and your prayers, They are you interpreting what's going on around you as your intuition helps you know what is new for you and needs some sorting. And so, as a favor in this appendix, I am handing you some thoughtful ways of moving forward.

Please remember, these are the tools that worked for me. You must choose your own.

Some Non-Physical Tools to Assist You!

Your Light!

I now understand that there is light inside of every one of us. It's even been proven. (Read Bruce Lipton or Gregg Braden). Light is energy. It also happens to be Divine. It's in your DNA and has the powerful ability to heal, create, manifest, sustain and express you. At times it is not working because it's been forgotten, like when you're totally down on yourself or being very judgmental.

Once you've cleared some of those issues and are thinking in a very positive way your light will show up, I've even SEEN my light from time to time. It's been when my energy is up and I am vibrating with some wonderful passion or new idea. It shows up and then it is a tool for me to literally use. With my imagination and trust, I can move this (my) Divine light around to relieve pain in my body, send healing, create or expand my being, create a design, or even write a book! It is yours to use on you or others. Even use it to heal the planet. Please use it to heal the planet.

Another thing that helps it show up is by believing it will. You must practice using it. When I used to play tennis, for example, if I twisted my ankle or stubbed my toe I would stop for a moment and just imagine great light moving into the spot. The pain would vanish. Use it! Practice using it!

A beautiful story a friend shared with me about light goes like this: Jack was three and a half. He had misbehaved and it upset him so he disappeared. His mother searched and searched and finally found him hiding under the dining room table. She asked him what was wrong. "I don't like who I am," he said.

His wise mother sat him on her knee, and told him, "Jack, there is a light inside of you! You know that toy of yours that has a light inside? There's a light inside of you that looks just like that, and you can use it to shift that feeling about yourself!"

Ever since that moment, Jack has remembered the message. He'll suddenly say to his mother, "Mommy, I'm thinking about that light inside of me."

Oh how I wish someone had said that to me when I was three and a half, and that I was half as smart as Jack.

Your Thoughts!

Your thoughts are what manifest everything in your life. It's as simple as that. I hardly have to say more, except I will mention that when you're thinking something isn't going to work, it is as powerful, as when you're thinking that something is going to work. Consider this an important statement!

If you want to explore thoughts, the books of Abraham by Esther and Jerry Hicks are the best I've found.

Your Beliefs!

Your beliefs impact your thoughts, no matter how intelligent you are, or what great work you're reading. If you have a contrary belief, you will not accept new material. This may keep you very stuck! Sometimes beliefs need therapy to shift them. We're not always aware of those lurking demons against worthiness, deserving, and possibilities.

I will suggest that you suspend your beliefs as you read this book. You can make that choice right in the moment by just deciding that for now you choose to accept this story as absolutely possible. Being open keeps possibilities and thinking flowing. You may come back and decide it's all hogwash, but at least you gave the idea a change to be considered.

Doing Meditation

The meditative state is a state of being that you achieve with practice. It serves you tremendously for you'll move toward a peace, clarity, and calmness. It can be you sitting very still with a peaceful mind, or you totally absorbed in a process such as painting, writing, sewing, sculpting, or doing some form of yoga or movement. That is when your mind is empty of chatter, worry, anger, and deliberation. Peace has a chance to move in! I sometimes see purple and a yellow green when I've reached a deep state of meditation. It helps me be in touch with my progress.

Meditation may already be your everyday practice. That's great if it is! It will enhance your journey. It is a subtle tool and takes discipline just to sit down and do it. If sitting still, peacefully and comfortably is the form you choose, then empty your mind and focus on your breath whenever and wherever it feels good for as long as you wish. You can even do it in waiting rooms and airline terminals. Focusing on a particular word, such as "peace," or an image of something you cherish works.

Your mind will absolutely resist being emptied, but the breath will assist if you diligently follow it, breathing in, breathing out.

Some instructions suggest that you ask the question who am I? Why am I here? What do I want?

I once was advised to change my beginning question. "You now know who you are, so you muddle everything. Move to asking "what is my next step?" Questions can also focus on exploring the answer regarding some synchronicity, or sighting that you've experienced or decision that needs to be made. Answers may not come during the meditation, but rest assured that they will come, and when they do you may want to journal. The messages will help you SEE AND FEEL your journey! There are as many good books as there are approaches to meditation.

Your Journaling

I'm sure you've used journaling, but if you have not, it is amazing how it can lead you along to some very deep feelings, awareness or answers about yourself or an encounter in your life. There are times when I am personally hurting, and I'm not in touch with the real reason. If I just start writing non-stop, writing everything that comes into my mind, whether nice or not, all of the sudden I'm putting words on paper that are new to me, thoughts that tell me some very powerful things.

Your Praying

I once read that prayer is a naked reach for God. In prayer we can strip away the dogma, the flowery words, the superficial and put out what we want. I've always loved the writing of Malcolm Boyd, In his book, *Are You Running With Me Jesus*, he suggests that we speak our prayers in real words and sentences, and sentiments for that matter that come completely from our hearts (our guts really) as if we were talking to our best friend (which we are).

The science of prayer is to not say "I want to be well," but instead "I celebrate my wellness with gratitude," as though it has already come to be. Gregg Braden's book, *Secrets of the Lost Mode of Prayer*, is excellent at presenting this theory.

Peter Roche de Coppen, a philosopher and author of many books, claims that whenever he's "off" his wife tells him to go and pray. He says it always works, and that he would not be where he is today, without it.

Your Laughter

This may seem a strange tool, but it is not. I'm sure you've heard the term "the lightness of being." It's essential, to hold off rigidity, an overly serious attitude, and inflexibility, not to forget humor.

I added this tool when one day I looked out of the window and observed a magnificent Downy Woodpecker holding onto a very thin, floppy, twig-like branch and bouncing about in a ridiculous manner. It went on and on and brought me to my knees laughing.

My history with the mirror outside my window told me to examine whether I was being a bit uptight, and I was! Time to loosen up and enjoy the process

Your Faith

This is about *your* faith in yourself. You're sorting possibilities of what is. You really need faith in your ability to do this, to acknowledge your history, your stuckness, and your ability to change, and your willingness to stay with what you do believe. Important!

Your Love and Acceptance

There's probably nothing more powerful than your own love and acceptance of yourself and All. It is a constant process of witnessing your thoughts, feelings, and all judgments and plain old caring. In fact it starts with the caring and builds to feeling the love. If you keep on being honest with yourself and others (the highest form of caring) you will begin to feel good and feeling the love!

Trust

Sometimes just saying to yourself that you know this is going to work, you know you have the potential, and you know you are a magnificent being will build a trust that will supersede all doubt.

Ritual

Ritual is when you set aside some time to go through your own physical motions that emphasize to you the sacredness of who you are, or what you're doing. It can be as simple as touching your heart as you leave your home or taking in something sacred. You might burn something to signify that you're letting go, or lay a flower in a stream. Then there's dancing in moonlight holding your intention, especially on the Full Moon!

Objects, music, chanting, movement, words, candlelight, incense, affirmations, or anything that is beloved to you can be used in ritual. Doing a ritual creates an aura, focusing you and the energy around you. It acknowledges the Divine Presence in your life.

I bought the original painting, which has become the cover of this book, at an exhibit of young artists held at Alex Grey's gallery. They shipped it to me by Fed Ex, and it arrived just now (That's what I mean about everything in your life beginning to align.) A ritual about its significance to me needed to happen right in this moment.

I was delighted with how powerful to have found and bought this painting. I was in such a deep place about receiving the box in this particular moment. Ritual was perfect to really impound the sacredness. I lit a candle. I opened the box; I held the framed art piece in my hands in silence, experiencing its power and beauty. I felt grateful to the artist, Mary Myrka, and appreciated the media she'd used (Caran d' Ache.) Ritual and gratitude assisted me to experience this moment as fully as possible. This is the greatness of ritual.

It's why we have wedding ceremonies, baby blessings and baptisms, graduations, and funerals, to honor the sacredness of the moment.

Dreams.

Your dreams can often act as an oracle giving you guidance or input. A story that illustrates this quite well is a dream I had when I was struggling about whether to have surgery. Doctors felt that a nodule on my thyroid should be removed. I was very healthy and questioned the need for surgery. Then I had a dream of very special friends of mine, a car, and an Irish Setter named "Taos." The dream made no sense to me, so I trusted that I would someday understand it.

Months later I was in New Mexico for a workshop. A couple who had registered for the same workshop called and invited my friend, Carol and me to dinner to get acquainted. We met in the bar and went on to a restaurant. Our conversation went deep very quickly, and I found myself talking about the decision regarding my thyroid. This person chose to be quite direct in response to my story. He said, "You look extremely healthy to me. Perhaps what's in your body is perfectly normal to you. You could choose to trust that all is well for you."

I thanked him for the input and mentally stored it in my file of many opinions, but not for long. Driving back to the hotel we swerved to miss hitting a dog. In the headlights its' eyes looked like stars with light exploding from them. I gulped. The dog was an Irish setter, and we were in Taos just like in my dream! I knew I would not have the surgery. All was well.

I suggest as you get answers, enter them in your journal under "What I've Asked For and Received." Date them and record your feelings. You'll finally receive so much that you'll no longer record it. Living this process is rich and what spirituality is about. Alex Grey says that opening subjectively to an internal experience of the sacred, (is) an opening to ultimate reality that will positively affect your mind and heart." **Trust it!**

Physical Tools to Assist You!

Personal Space

Some persons have one very special place (a Sacred Space) that is their spot of meditation, reading, journaling, and reflecting. To enhance the Sacred Spaces they add visuals such as pictures or crystals which help to focus experience. If you're creating a space be sure there's comfort, a feeling of safety, good light, candles or favorite objects, and your own blessing.

An Altar

All of us have altars, but we just aren't aware of them as "altars." They might be the refrigerator with pictures, your dresser, or even the rear view mirror in your car (I love to see what some people dangle there!) That may be enough. But you may decide you want to create a new altar; some place more specific.

The purpose of an altar is to take you within visually, to be a visual reminder about your life, and process. Consider the items that will help so that when you stand in front of your altar you are deeply moved and reminded. Candlelight might be useful or just placing something so sun hits it dramatically.

You may choose to have your altar in your meditation space. One friend has an altar on the windowsill at her kitchen sink. It's made up of glass objects that she's gathered over many years. Some have been gifts and some are things she's fallen in love with. Because they are glass they are enhanced by natural light during the day and indirect light at night. It's gorgeous!

Another friend has a portable altar. This altar consists of objects that are precious personally, wrapped in a beautiful piece of soft leather and tied with a leather lace. He carries it with him when he travels. He's never without it.

A Journal.

This book of empty pages is going to be used big time, so choose something that feels good to hold, one you like visually, one whose pages turn well, and you can write in easily and often. Choose one that makes you want to journal!

A Writing Tool

This may sound silly to you, but I have found being deliberate in all of my choices, even the choice of what I'm going to use to write is important. Choose a pen or pencil that feels good, and writes smoothly. This formalizes your project, and is you creating good support.

Oracles

An oracle is something that helps you interpret or understand your energy or your experience. Many of your oracles are the beings or objects that appear on your path such as my owl. There are also oracles that can help you interpret encounters, such as: runes, cards, the I Ching, and books. I don't use oracles every day, but I try to be aware of signs that need interpreting. I can find them in some wonderful books such as:

Jamie Sames – <u>Medicine Cards</u>
Jamie Sames – <u>Sacred Path Cards</u>
Ted Andrews – <u>Animal Speak</u>
Ted Andrews – <u>Nature Speak</u>
Doreen Virtue – <u>Messages From Angels</u>
Ralph Blum – <u>The Book of Runes</u>
The Tarot Cards
Kathy Tyler and Joy Drake - Original Angel Cards

My First Experience with Oracles

It is believed that your energy mingles with the energies of the oracle and brings forth very personal information. Years ago, I was in a beautiful, old temple in Taiwan. There were lines of people standing in line in front of me, who seemed priest-like. I was curious about what they were doing, so I found a spot and privately watched with great intensity. As each person arrived at the front of this line, he or she was given a handful of sticks, which they held in prayer and then dropped to the ground at the feet of the interpreter. The seer studied the configuration of the sticks and delivered the message that he saw. The line moved slowly and confidently.

I was mesmerized and soon after, out of curiosity, turned to my own oracles for help in understanding my life. I was comfortable with either choosing to accept the message, or deciding it did not apply. Over time I've met persons who hold the oracle with great superstition and fear. In my own life I consider the words it offers to be possibilities, and a choice.

Summary

All of these tools are only suggestions. Use any or all. For instance I needed oracles in the beginning to help me understand and interpret all that was happening. They were very beneficial. I now trust my feelings. My deepest growth has come from that trusting. And it took a while to get there!

Another Powerful Tool -

Sharing the Stories of Your Journey In A Group

For seven years I facilitated a group doing exactly this work. We'd gather every other week, and share stories from our everyday lives that needed telling, both joyful, and sad. We did exercises to help interpret or expose life understanding and to assist us in moving forward with our lives.

The participants were women who had been studying with me in design classes for a long time. They really wanted to continue working together, so we began a group titled "Designing Your Life." We confidently explored our lives, our signs, our stories, our need to change, grow and find joy. It was rich for all of us. Many of the exercises from those seven years are included in this book.

You may decide to form such a group and use this book as your source of inspiration to process your lives. The advantage is having others with whom you can share your thoughts. Everyone has a perspective and sharing can give you a new slant on an issue that's "up." I advise you read the book simultaneously and do the exercises as they are suggested with each chapter. Listening to each other and getting input on your discoveries will be significant and joyful.

I've always believed in sharing personal stories. Stories are such a part of our heritage. In fact it's how news was spread long ago. Today telling stories is being used in profound ways, especially with veterans who carry within them horrific experiences of war that are blocking their living and being abilities. Facilitators of this process are titled "Medical Anthropologists." They work in groups and encourage these ex-soldiers to tell their experiences of war in great detail, perhaps more than one time. The therapy is having huge success for it releases haunting moments that have been locked inside the psyche too long. The success is as the healing happens and the personal life moves forward.

We all need to be aware of this tool. You may find it's just perfect for you. Experiment with the group process idea, if your wish. And if you do so, let me know how it works!

CPSIA information can be obtained at www.ICGtesting.com
Printed in the USA
BVOW070841170412

287816BV00001B/1/P